P9-DVA-740

# Sonoma

# Sonoma

## The Ultimate Winery Guide

Revised and Updated, Second Edition

BY HEIDI H. CUSICK-DICKERSON

Preface by Rodney Strong
Foreword by John Ash

PHOTOGRAPHS BY RICHARD GILLETTE

CHRONICLE BOOKS

SAN FRANCISCO

Copyright © 1995 and 2005 by Heidi H. Cusick-Dickerson.
Photographs copyright © 1995 and 2005 by Richard Gillette.
All rights reserved. No part of this book may be reproduced in
any form without written permission from the publisher.

Library of Congress Cataloging-in-Publication Data available.

ISBN: 0-8118-4200-2

Manufactured in China

Designed by Susan Park

Distributed in Canada by Raincoast Books
9050 Shaughnessy Street
Vancouver, British Columbia V6P6E5

10 9 8 7 6 5 4 3 2 1

Chronicle Books LLC
85 Second Street
San Francisco, California 94105

www.chroniclebooks.com

## Dedication

We dedicate this book to Sonoma's vintners and farmers, with respect and admiration for the excellent fruits of their endeavors, and to all our wine-loving friends, for their continuous love and support.

—Heidi & Richard

# Acknowledgments

With heartfelt appreciation for John Gaston Dickerson, Shannon, Brendan, Lara, Bob, the late Irma, Sally, Lee, and Joan, Nancy and Rosemary, my fellow Adobe Artists, all of whose love, support, and wisdom nurture and sustain me. Thanks, too, to winemaker John Buechsenstein, Jamie Douglas of the Sonoma Winegrowers, Sheila Walker of Sonoma Tourism, and copy editor Carolyn Keating. To John Ash and Rodney Strong for their current and continued endorsement of my projects. And for all my family, current and ex, and friends in Mendocino and Sonoma counties.

—Heidi

With thanks to my daughters Jasara and Holly and grandchildren Zachary Martin and Natalie Lynn, Sandra McMahon, Dan and Bonnie Borghi, Shanti Finnerty, Chuck and Camille Hathaway, and the rest of my Mendocino family.

—Richard

# Contents

# Preface

To the east of the great breakers and foaming surf of the Pacific Ocean lies Sonoma County. Nestled between the bracing maritime air and the warm crests of the Mayacamas Mountains, this magnificent and unique cradle is one of the best places in the world to produce great wines. That's what this beautiful book is about—the sensual delights of a rare place and the welcome it extends to you, the visitor and native alike.

The grape has been intertwined with humanity for centuries—each enhancing the quality of the other.

The winegrowers of Sonoma County are diverse and eclectic in the pursuit of their art. The variance of climate in these small valleys, as the cool of the ocean collides with the warmth of the interior, allows winemakers to fine-tune their efforts to a degree unavailable in any other place. The early ripening grapes, such as Chardonnay and Pinot Noir, may live in the cool, redwood-scented banks of the Russian River—with the salty perfume of the sea air streaming over the passes between the coastal hills—and the cool nights of the gravelly loam plateaus. Big, feral Cabernet Sauvignon can be realized in the warmer regions of the Dry Creek and Alexander valleys. Zinfandel and Sauvignon Blanc excel by moving a few kilometers in either direction toward the yin and yang of the sea and the hills.

It is all of this that we want to share with you. Salmon run in the streams; sheep graze on the headlands; cheese, fresh vegetables, and wildflowers abound; and rare serendipities surround you in a cornucopia of pleasure. For those of you who have not yet tasted the pleasures of this place, we encourage you to use this book as a catalyst for adventure and personal gratification. The vines, the colors of their leaves, the yeasty smells of wine in ferment, and the excitement of your own personal discoveries await you in Sonoma County.

I came here in 1959 and have planted many grapes. I've pruned them and worried over them, and in return I have accepted their treasure. There is nothing better. I will travel, but I will never leave. I am here. Join me.

—**Rodney Strong**
*Sonoma County Grape Grower and Winemaker*

# Foreword

As I thought about what to write for this foreword, I looked back on the original edition that Heidi did in 1995. I was struck by how much has changed in the wine business in Sonoma in that short ten-year period of time. The number of wineries has increased substantially, as has the variety of grapes being grown and made into wine. Appellation designations have also increased, reminding us of the extraordinary diversity that lies in this county of almost sixteen hundred square miles.

Sonoma is arguably the most varied of all the North Coast wine-growing areas. From the volcanic highlands of the Mayacamas Mountains in the east to the magnificent, wind-whipped and wave-washed Pacific shore, Sonoma's diversity of climate and soils is what makes it one of the greatest areas in the world to grow wine grapes.

Sonoma County has a rich agricultural as well as social history. For thousands of years the county's abundant natural resources supported three distinct Indian tribes—the Coast Miwok, Pomo, and Wappo. Though only remnants remain of these native tribes, they taught and set the stage for the European and American settlers who followed. Each of these in turn has contributed to Sonoma's special flavor in the last few centuries. Sonoma has seen six flags raised over its soil, those of England, Spain, Russia, Mexico, the United States, and the Bear Flag Republic. Many of these early settlers brought with them a love of food and wine, and the seeds that they planted continue to grow and thrive today.

When I first visited Sonoma in the late 1960s I knew I had to live here. I was still in college, but felt like I had stumbled into a cook's paradise. There were fresh salmon, Dungeness crab, and other seafood abundantly available from Bodega Bay, as well as dairy and poultry from all parts of the county, especially from around Petaluma. There were fruits and vegetables of many varieties, along with sheep, cows, and wild foods including mushrooms, greens, and, of course, game. I couldn't (and still can't) wait for the wild blackberries that ripen in mid to late summer. They are for me the harbinger of the grape harvest and a sign that it will soon be starting the cycle resulting in that magical beverage called wine!

To visit Sonoma during the grape harvest is to experience a light and smell that doesn't exist in any other part of the world—even in the neighboring counties of Napa and Mendocino. I can't put my finger on exactly why this is, but many who have come to visit me here exclaim that they've never seen more beautiful sunsets or experienced more enticing and unique aromas and tastes. To slow down and reconnect with the most basic senses is to experience a relationship that many of us have forgotten in the daily rush and activity of our lives. That may be the real magic of Sonoma.

Heidi and Richard are unique in their ability to capture a sense of what Sonoma and its wines are all about. I applaud them for their vision. I'm sure this will become an essential guidebook for all who travel here. We look forward to sharing our little piece of heaven with you!

—John Ash
*Sonoma County Chef*

 # Introduction

# Introduction

Sonoma County's grape harvest begins with coastal Chardonnay picked near old-growth redwoods on cool, sepia mornings. It continues with Pinot Noir clipped in the tepid warmth of oak-studded valleys, and climaxes when Cabernet clusters are cut from steep heat-trapped terraces. Sonoma County, the birthplace of American viticulture, encompasses the most diverse cross section of geography in the California wine country.

Highway 101, Sonoma's marketing link to the rest of the world, divides the county down the middle. Any exit in any direction leads within minutes to a rural mix of beauty and business. As you visit, you'll find that the owners and tasting room personnel take pride in their regions and in the American Viticultural Areas in which their wine is produced. There are eleven designated AVAs in Sonoma County. Following the French, AVAs are the U.S. designations of wine-growing areas, identified by their particular climate and geography. For example, the AVA known as Los Carneros, a Spanish name for the sheep that graze here, stretches across the southern end of both Sonoma and Napa Counties, on San Pablo Bay. Pinot Noir and Chardonnay grapes grow best in this flat, windy region.

It's logical to begin your Sonoma County wine tour in the Carneros at the southeastern end of the county. You'll find this to be as much a historical jaunt as it is a wine experience. California's story of winemaking begins in the town of Sonoma, where history and food blend with the wine and natural beauty.

You can stay at the charming El Dorado Hotel right on the Plaza or Ramekins Bed and Breakfast, next to General Mariano Guadalupe Vallejo's home. Both exemplify Sonoma's food and wine connection. El Dorado is located above Piatti's Italian restaurant and across the street from the acclaimed "the girl & the fig" restaurant. In addition to being an inn, Ramekins is also a cooking school where the best cooks use a plethora of Sonoma-grown ingredients. One of those ingredients is olives, which have been planted in such abundance that a three-month festival takes place after the winter harvest every year. The Olive Festival begins with a blessing of the olives and includes tastings and special events throughout Sonoma Valley.

Across from Sonoma's central plaza is the Mission San Francisco de Solano. Here in 1824, the Spanish priest Father Altimira planted grapes for sacramental wine. After the secularization of the mission, General Vallejo acquired the vineyards and, in 1841, made the first commercial wine north of San Francisco from those vines. Because the mission grapes didn't make great-tasting wine, premium winemaking had to wait for the local producers to use other varietals they were bringing in from Europe and from nurseries on the East Coast, which were also importing cuttings from Europe. In 1856, Agoston Haraszthy, an Austro-Hungarian exile, imported a hundred thousand grape cuttings from Europe and sold them all over California from his winery, Buena Vista. His and his son's marketing efforts wrote the history of Haraszthy's significance in the industry, but there were many other family grape growers at the time. Most worked as farmers in the growing season and vintners after harvest, just like at many wineries today in Sonoma County. Two-thirds of the wineries profiled here are family owned.

North of Sonoma, above tiny Glen Ellen on Sonoma Mountain, is Jack London State Park. The Valley of the Moon, as Sonoma Valley is known, was immortalized by London's book of the same name. The name came from the local Miwoks, who called Sonoma Valley "valley of the moons" because the moon seemed to set several times over the mountain peaks.

Continuing north, Highway 12 passes wineries, restaurants, and vineyards as it traverses Sonoma Valley, nestled between the Mayacamas and Sonoma mountains. Along this route another famous author, M. F. K. Fisher, spent her last years in an adobe-style house adjacent to the Bouverie Audubon Preserve.

The narrow, busy road bisects the county from the Napa border to Bodega Bay, and passes through Santa Rosa, Sonoma's business, cultural, and marketing hub. It was here in 1875 that a winemaking commune, based on a utopian spiritualism called Swedenborgianism, was founded. Until Prohibition a Scotsman, Thomas Lake Harris, and his protégé Kanaye Nagasawa made wine from Cabernet Sauvignon, Riesling, and Zinfandel grapes next to the Fountaingrove Round Barn, which is visible from Highway 101, as it sits on a knoll overlooking the city at the north end of town.

Famed horticulturist Luther Burbank lived in Santa Rosa for fifty years. His gardens and home, a few blocks from downtown, are open to visitors. Gold Ridge Farm, his nursery twelve miles away in Sebastopol, sells plants year-round. Nearby, the Sonoma County Fairgrounds hosts the county fair in July and the Harvest Festival, a prestigious wine and food awards gala, in September. A growing number of fine restaurants are found in Santa Rosa, many in the downtown area near Fourth Street and others around the old Railroad Square on the west side of Highway 101. The wine list at Equus, the restaurant on Mendocino Avenue at the foot of the Fountaingrove Round Barn, features nearly every winery in Sonoma County. John Ash & Co. at Vintners Inn, in the vineyards northwest of Santa Rosa, is one of the nation's top restaurants and a central spot to stay for a few nights.

To the west of Santa Rosa along Highway 12, you pass apple orchards, berry farms, and horse pastures on the way to the coast. In a region known for its Gravensteins, the apple-growing heritage is celebrated with a fair in Sebastopol every August. Sebastopol's main street is a mix of Victorian gingerbread and 1950s functional architecture. Several cappuccino parlors and bookstores are worth a stop, and antique hounds will love the southern stretch of Highway 116.

On the coast, Bodega Bay is still a busy fishing port. To the south on the Sonoma-Marin County border are the oyster beds of Tomales Bay. Going up Coast Highway One, you'll come to Fort Ross, where in 1812 a hundred Russians established the first European settlement this side of San Francisco. They also planted the first grapes north of San Francisco with cuttings carried from the Black Sea. Thirty miles south of Fort Ross is the mouth of the great Russian River. Cutting a swath through Sonoma County, it is a source of irrigation water, gravel, recreational activity, and environmental controversy. Most important for viticulture, the river creates a conduit for fog and the tempering effect of the Pacific, leading to the long, favorable growing season in which many grape varietals thrive.

Sparkling wine grapes do well along the Russian River, as the three Korbel brothers discovered in the mid-1870s. More *méthode champenoise* wine comes from the Russian River than anywhere else in California. Years ago, the Northwestern Pacific Railway brought vacationers from San Francisco to Occidental, Guerneville, and Forestville, three Russian River region towns that have been preserved as they were in an earlier era. Occidental's old hotels, the Negri and the Union, still serve family-style Italian dinners just as they have since 1924. Along the river itself you'll find cabins looking like they did at the beginning of the Depression and shops with crafts that haven't changed since the 1960s. Osmosis mineral baths in Freestone, however, bring spa lovers to bask in soothing enzymes away from it all.

To the north, redwood forests give way to a fringe of pine and oak trees. Before grapes, hops were the main crop in Dry Creek Valley. A few hop kilns are still situated around the area, the most notable being the one that houses Hop Kiln Winery. In the late 1800s the temperate climate of the Dry Creek and Alexander Valleys attracted Italian immigrants, who felt at home on the rolling, grassy hills and fertile river banks. They planted plums, peaches, and grapes and made bulk wines to truck to San Francisco neighborhoods. The defunct Italian-Swiss Colony in Asti started out in 1881 as an agricultural commune designed to help immigrants earn their own land by working it. In 1912 the colony produced three million gallons of wine; at one time it was the largest winery in California. (See the profile on Seghesio Family Vineyards on page 86 for their connection to the Italian Swiss Colony.) Nine of the wineries profiled here carry on their Italian heritage and traditions.

Today one of the largest wineries in the world, E. J. Gallo, known here as Gallo Sonoma, is making premium wine from grapes grown on thousands of acres in the county. The sculpted vineyards you see along Highway 101 south of Cloverdale and north of Petaluma are Gallo's. Their fashionable tasting room is a trendy stop on the Plaza in Healdsburg. Tasting is done in flights of wine at intimate tables in the sit-down scene. The winery is located at the historic Frei Ranch in Dry Creek Valley, but isn't open to the public.

When it comes to food, Healdsburg is one of northern California's meccas. In addition to restaurants, bakeries, Victorian buildings, bed-and-breakfast inns, and several winery tasting rooms, name brands like Charlie Palmer with his Dry Creek Kitchen, Ralph Tingle at Bistro Ralph, and protégés from Chez Panisse like Kathleen Sullivan from Downtown Bakery add to the draw. The plaza in the middle of town hosts concerts, wine tastings, and other community events, and is a place to picnic as well.

Geyserville is a quiet town named for the steamy sources of power in the hills to the east. You can find fine dining here at Santi, as well as a tasting room called Locals that features hard-to-find small family producers. There is also a variety of lodging choices, from the Hope Merrill bed-and-breakfast inns to Isis Oasis Lodge, which pays tribute to Egyptian gods and customs.

Now that Highway 101, with its burden of trucks, bypasses Cloverdale, Sonoma's northern gateway is recovering its small-town charm. Orange trees grow well in this hot microclimate, and have been the theme of the annual Citrus Fair since 1892. Good restaurants and a visitor's center have become part of the amenities. And the prestigious San Francisco Chronicle Wine Competition is held in Cloverdale each year.

Sonoma County is a picnic-lover's haven, especially at the sites maintained by wineries. More than two-thirds of the wineries profiled here provide picnic tables. And many have Sonoma-made cheeses, condiments, and bread and crackers available for spontaneous picnics. The wineries that don't have provisions are close to sources that do, such as Oakville Grocery, Downtown Bakery, and the Healdsburg Charcuterie in Healdsburg; Traverso's in Santa Rosa; Sonoma Jack Cheese Co., Vella's Cheese, and Sonoma Saveurs in Sonoma; Dry Creek General Store in Dry Creek; and the renowned Jimtown Store in Alexander Valley.

Although every winery in Sonoma County has its particular visitor appeal, each of the wineries featured here was chosen for its outstanding historical, architectural, and consumer-oriented features. And each exemplifies the hospitality and winemaking for which Sonoma County is known. The wineries are grouped by location in the southern, northern, and western geographical areas of the county. If you would like to group your visit into manageable stops for a day's jaunt, see the suggested Triangle Tours, page 28.

I selected these wineries on the basis of years of my own touring and on the recommendations of friends, colleagues, and other winery visitors I've met along the way. Sonoma has changed since this book was first written, and this edition reflects those changes. Every effort has been made to make sure the information given here was accurate at press time. Tasting room hours, fees, and tours are subject to change. If you have your heart set on a winery event, tour, or tasting, it's best to call ahead or check the website to avoid disappointment. In accordance with the Americans with Disabilities Act, except where historically impossible, these wineries are accessible to everyone. It is advisable to call ahead for specifics.

Having grown up in the San Francisco Bay Area, I first visited Sonoma wineries on Sunday drives with my parents and siblings. At twenty-one, I headed to Buena Vista, California's first winery. That tour and tasting in the old cellar launched my passion for Sonoma wineries, and my twenty-plus years as a resident of neighboring Mendocino County have allowed me to continue exploring the pleasures of Sonoma Country. I invite you to join me.

"I firmly believe, from what I have seen, that this is the chosen spot of all this earth as far as Nature is concerned."

Luther Burbank
1849 – 1926

# The Sonoma Food Connection

If it takes food to make a wine region great, Sonoma County is right there at the top. Many things have changed since I first wrote this book in 1995, but not Sonoma County's natural affinity for raising good things to eat and drink, as the early Pomos, Wappos, and Miwoks knew long before the Europeans and Asians arrived.

"The soil here is so good. It's volcanic ash, you know. People taste more of the wines than the food right now, but it's the same thing. You don't go where there is bad soil and raise good food," said the late doyenne of food writing M. F. K. Fisher, in remarks about living in Sonoma.

Wine grapes have been raised next to vegetables, fruits, and farm animals in Sonoma County since the Russians settled at Fort Ross in 1812. A dozen years later, when the Spanish missionaries came to Sonoma Valley, they planted olive trees, vegetables, wheat, and three thousand grapevines. The Italian immigrants brought more of the same when they settled in the northern part of the county. Their influence continues to be found in a third of the wineries profiled here.

As you visit wineries throughout the county, you'll see vegetable farms, olive and fruit orchards, goat and sheep dairies, cattle ranches, poultry processors, mushroom cultivators, and roadside produce stands interspersed among nearly sixty thousand acres of vineyards. It's no surprise that Sonoma County is known as California's "Provence."

Various regions in the county are known for what they grow. The southwest, around Petaluma, is dairy and poultry country. The land is rich in natural grass for grazing and for raising feed. In 1920, Petaluma was shipping four million pounds of butter a year and had three of the largest creameries in the West. Dairies still process their milk in Petaluma, home to Clover-Stornetta Farms, cre-

ator of Clo, the famous billboard cow. In downtown Petaluma, with its Victorian buildings along the riverfront, restaurants and creameries abound. Nearby, the Marin French Cheese Company straddles the county line and makes the popular Rouge et Noir cheeses.

Often referred to as the "chicken capital of the world," Petaluma, home of Rocky the Range Chicken, celebrates its heritage with an annual Butter & Egg Days Parade and festival in April. Ducks are another Petaluma specialty. Reichardt Duck Farms and Liberty Farm supply more than a million premium ducks a year to high-end grocers and the best restaurants in the country. "Old-fashioned nitrite-free" smoked chicken, duck, goose, turkey, and pheasant come from Pietrowski Smoked Poultry. And Petaluma is also renowned for the gigantic pumpkin farm and corn maze that slows the pace of Highway 101 travelers in the fall.

In western Sonoma County, the remnants of the once-booming apple industry survive in Sebastopol, which still celebrates its heritage with the annual Gravenstein Apple Fair held every year in August. Just outside of town at Gold Ridge Farm, Luther Burbank's Sebastopol nursery, Burbank developed more than 800 plants, including 113 new varieties of plums and prunes.

Near Sebastopol, along the Gravenstein Highway, you'll find farm stands and Mom's Apple Pies. On the Occidental Road, excellent goat cheese and a tour of the dairy are worth a stop at Redwood Hill Farm. Exotic

mushrooms became accessible on a regular basis to chefs and markets when Malcolm Clark started farming shiitakes and oyster mushrooms in a warehouse near Graton. And Willie Bird's turkeys come from this part of the county.

Berries are big business in the Russian River region. Kozlowski Farms on the Gravenstein Highway carries fresh berries and apples in season, plus a mouthwatering line of preserves and condiments. Nearby on Ross Station Road, Green Valley Farm has fresh blueberries plus ice cream, shakes, and muffins in the summer. Both farms are on the way to Iron Horse Vineyards.

Northern Sonoma was once a major supplier of hops to the beer industry. Grapes and produce grow in former hop fields near the Russian River, where Hop Kiln Winery is a beautiful reminder of old times. A renaissance in microbrewing has brought at least eight breweries to the county, including Bear Republic in Healdsburg, Powerhouse in Sebastopol, Russian River Brewing Company and Third Street Aleworks in Santa Rosa, and Moonlight in Windsor.

Alexander Valley used to be filled with prune, peach, and pear trees where vines now thrive. Today, Jimtown Store is a destination to pick up many of Sonoma's locally made cheeses, bread, condiments, and more for your winery picnic. Once a sleepy farm town, Geyserville has blossomed into a culinary oasis. Restaurants like Santi and the Alexander Valley Grille at Chateau Souverain beckon like *auberges* in southern France.

Olives are becoming big business in Sonoma County. In addition to having prizewinning wine, B.R. Cohn on the Sonoma Highway led the rebirth in olive production in Sonoma County. Many of the wineries and small growers have their olives pressed at the Olive Mill in Glen Ellen, a shop and working mill that is a destination for olive lovers. Nicholas Turkey Breeders, the largest turkey breeder in the United States, is in the neighborhood, next door to Gundlach-Bundschu Winery.

Ten years ago there were about half a dozen excellent cheese producers who called Sonoma County home. Two, Vella Cheese Company and Sonoma Cheese Factory, have been making cow's milk cheese since the early 1930s.

Laura Chenel, who pioneered the manufacturing of American goat cheese in 1980 in Santa Rosa, makes her cheese near the town of Sonoma. An increasing number of producers offer an astounding variety of fresh, aged, and handcrafted cow, goat, and sheep's milk cheeses.

Sonoma County is also known for its lamb and beef, which on the hoof graze the hillsides around Healdsburg, Sonoma, and Petaluma. And every town has at least one bakery specializing in excellent French, organic, or specially flavored crusty loaves of bread.

As you go from winery to winery, you'll also notice many small produce markets and farm stands along the way. When I first wrote this guide, I included nearby food and farm stands with each winery. Since then the food has moved into the tasting rooms. I urge you to get a Sonoma County Farm Trails (see Resources) map to locate those that are open for visits and sales. Seventeen of the wineries in this guide have Sonoma-made cheese, olive oil, condiments, meats, and other edibles to purchase as a memento or for a spontaneous picnic. Thirteen of the wineries have significant ongoing educational food and wine programs that are worth reserving a space in if desired.

In Sonoma County, food and wine festivals abound. These include the Olive Festival in Sonoma, a Seafood Festival in Bodega Bay, the Harvest Fair in Santa Rosa, the Apple Blossom Festival in Sebastopol, Citrus Fair in Cloverdale, and the Butter & Egg Days Parade in Petaluma. You'll also find wine-centric celebrations coordinated by the regional associations such as the Russian River Wine Road, Sonoma Valley Vintners, Alexander Valley Winegrowers, and Dry Creek Winegrowers (see Resources for contact information). Two big events, the Sonoma County Showcase of Wine & Food in July and the Sonoma Valley Auction on Labor Day weekend, herald Sonoma as a world-class wine and food region.

All around the United States, Sonoma-grown wine, poultry, apples, mushrooms, meats, fruit, and cheeses are labeled on menus. After touring Sonoma's wine country, the next time you see the Sonoma designation, you'll know why. It's another affirmation of the natural affinity Sonoma has with its food and wine.

# A Month-by-Month Guide to Winemaking

Grapes left on their own will begin to ferment as soon as their juices break out. Yeast present on the skin consumes natural sugar in the juice, producing alcohol and flavor compounds, and soon the grapes are on their way to becoming wine. Centuries ago this was how wine was discovered. It sounds simple, but many other factors, such as wild bacteria, changes in temperature, and incomplete fermentation, can affect the outcome. As the science and practical application of winemaking have advanced, so have the quality and control of the magical transition from grape juice into wine.

This brief month-by-month summary lets you know what is happening behind the tasting room where the finished products are shared. Basic treatments, such as racking, aging, filtering, and bottling, are included as they are typically applied during the winemaking process. As you tour the different wineries, you will discover individual approaches that differ from the norm. Learning about these differences will add to your appreciation of what goes into winemaking and personalize your enjoyment of each variation.

**AUGUST:** The harvest and crush begin, continuing into September, October, and sometimes November, depending on the year. Grapes for sparkling wines are harvested first, followed by white and red grapes for dry table wines. Cabernet Sauvignon and botrytised grapes for sweet wines are picked last.

**SEPTEMBER:** White grapes are picked, destemmed, and pressed to yield only juice. Cultured yeast may be added, and grapes begin fermentation in stainless-steel or wood containers. The optional addition (usually reserved for Chardonnay among the whites) of malolactic bacteria transforms the natural malic acid, which is tart, into lactic acid, which is more buttery and supple.

Red grapes are picked and optionally destemmed. The crushed grapes (skins, pulp, and juice) are pumped to a fermenter, where commercial yeast may be added. The grapes are fermented with their skins for varying amounts of time to pick up color; several times a day the cap of skins that rises to the top is punched down or pumped over to extract flavor and more color. In carbonic maceration, a different fermenta-

tion technique, whole clusters are enclosed in a container without air and allowed to ferment internally, as opposed to fermentation with yeast. Malolactic fermentation is common with red grapes. Pressing is done from one to four weeks after harvesting, depending on the style of the winemaker.

**OCTOBER:** Fermenting white grape juice samples (must) are tested in the laboratory to determine whether fermentation is complete. The fermenting must may be stirred to mix the lees, or remaining grape solids, into the juice for more flavor.

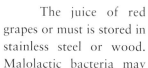

The juice of red grapes or must is stored in stainless steel or wood. Malolactic bacteria may be added now. Samples tested in the lab determine whether fermentation is complete.

**NOVEMBER:** Newly fermented juice may be stirred to incorporate settled lees into the wine. The clarification process begins by racking, that is, the drawing of wine from one tank into another container and leaving behind the natural sediment.

**DECEMBER:** This is a quiet time for the wine, which is stored in wood or stainless-steel containers for the next several months (the whites) or months to years (the reds). These may be stirred or racked, and wines from previous vintages may be filtered, blended, or bottled. Labels might be redesigned; labels and bottles are ordered when quantities are determined, and bottling dates are scheduled for the upcoming year.

**JANUARY:** Wines from last September's harvest continue developing in wood or stainless steel; samples are tested in the laboratory to determine acid and remaining sugar levels, and are tasted for flavor. Previous vintages may be filtered, blended, or bottled. Blends for sparkling wines (cuvées) may begin secondary fermentation combined with a mixture of yeast and sugar (which creates the bubble-producing fermentation), after which they are bottled and capped. Then they are left alone, except for occasional rotation, for one to three or more years.

**FEBRUARY:** Sweet wines from September's harvest can be filtered and bottled. Dry wines continue development in tanks and barrels. The racking of red wines continues. Grapes are contracted for the next harvest. Now or at any time of the year, the riddling of previous vintages of sparkling wine can begin. This periodic turning of each bottle moves

dead yeast cells and residue to the bottle necks, for eventual removal.

**MARCH:** White wines from oak barrels may be racked now and transferred to stainless-steel containers. The clarifying process continues by several different methods. Fining is the addition of a coagulating ingredient such as egg white (usually for reds) or the natural clay powder

bentonite (usually for whites), which floats through the wine, attracts suspended particles, and draws them to the bottom. When clarified by filtering, the wine is pumped through fine screens such as those made from cellulose fibers or diatomaceous earth, which remove yeast and particulate matter. Bottling usually takes place right after filtering.

**APRIL through JUNE:** The aging of red wines continues. White wines, and also red and white wines from previous vintages, can be fined, filtered, or both, and bottled as described above. Tanks are constantly washed and oak barrels scrubbed between uses. Previous vintages of sparkling wine can be disgorged. This is the process of freezing the bottle neck and popping off the cap to remove the dead yeast cells assembled at the cap through riddling. A dosage is then added. Dosage is a mixture of sugar and wine that determines whether the wine will be brut (the driest), extra dry, sec, or demi-sec (the sweetest). The wine is then corked, secured with wire, and covered with foil.

**JULY through AUGUST:** Wineries prepare for the harvest. Wines are shifted from stainless-steel and oak to other containers as necessary to allow room for new juice; new oak barrels are brought in; extra crew is hired; and grapes are sampled in the vineyard to determine sugar and acid levels. The bottling of previous vintages continues.

# Winery Tours

CHAMPAGNE/ SPARKLING WINE
Buena Vista Winery
  (tasting room only)
Chateau St. Jean
Gloria Ferrer Champagne Caves
Iron Horse Vineyards
J Vineyards & Winery
Korbel Champagne Cellars
Trentadue Winery

CONCERTS OR
THEATRICAL EVENTS
Buena Vista Winery
Field Stone Winery
Gloria Ferrer Champagne Caves
Gundlach-Bundschu Winery
Rodney Strong Vineyards

GARDENS
Alexander Valley Vineyards
Benziger Family Winery
Chateau St. Jean
Cline Cellars
Dry Creek Vineyard
Ferrari-Carano Vineyards
  & Winery
Matanzas Creek Winery
Preston of Dry Creek Winery
  & Vineyards
Seghesio Family Vineyards
Trentadue Winery
Viansa Winery & Italian
  Marketplace

HISTORICAL INTEREST
Alexander Valley Vineyards
Buena Vista Winery
Cline Cellars
Foppiano Vineyards
Gundlach-Bundschu Winery
Korbel Champagne Cellars
Sebastiani Vineyards & Winery
Simi Winery

LUNCH AND/OR
PICNIC PROVISIONS
Benziger Family Winery
Buena Vista Winery
Chateau St. Jean (has charcuterie)
Chateau Souverain (has restaurant)
Cline Cellars
Field Stone Winery

Geyser Peak Winery
Gloria Ferrer Champagne Caves
Gundlach-Bundschu Winery
Hop Kiln Winery
Korbel Champagne Cellars
  (has deli and market)
Preston of Dry Creek Winery
  & Vineyards
Ravenswood Winery
  (Sundays, June–October)
Rodney Strong Vineyards
Sebastiani Vineyards & Winery
  (on the Square in Sonoma)
Trentadue Winery
Viansa Winery & Italian
  Marketplace (has Italian deli-
  catessen at winery and in Sonoma)

NOTABLE FOOD AND/OR
WINE PROGRAMS
Buena Vista Winery
Chateau St. Jean
Chateau Souverain
Ferrari-Carano Vineyards & Winery
Geyser Peak Winery
Gloria Ferrer Champagne Caves
J Vineyards & Winery
Ravenswood Winery
St. Francis Winery & Vineyards
Sebastiani Vineyards & Winery
Simi Winery
Trentadue Winery
Viansa Winery & Italian
  Marketplace

OUTSTANDING ARCHITECTURE
Chateau St. Jean
Chateau Souverain
Ferrari-Carano Vineyards & Winery
Fritz Winery
Gloria Ferrer Champagne Caves
Hop Kiln Winery
J Vineyards & Winery

Rodney Strong Vineyards
St. Francis Winery & Vineyards
Viansa Winery & Italian
  Marketplace

OUTSTANDING PANORAMAS
Benziger Family Winery
  (on tram tour)
Chateau St. Jean (on tour from
  bell tower)
Chateau Souverain
Geyser Peak Winery
Gloria Ferrer Champagne Caves
Gundlach-Bundschu Winery
Iron Horse Vineyards
Viansa Winery & Italian
  Marketplace

OUTSTANDING TOURS
Benziger Family Winery
Buena Vista Winery
Chateau St. Jean
Chateau Souverain
Cline Cellars
Gloria Ferrer Champagne Caves
Korbel Champagne Cellars
Sebastiani Vineyards & Winery
Simi Winery
Trentadue Winery

SELF-GUIDED TOURS
Benziger Family Winery
Buena Vista Winery
Chateau St. Jean
Foppiano Vineyards
Matanzas Creek Winery
Sebastiani Vineyards & Winery
Viansa Winery & Italian
  Marketplace

VINEYARD VISITS
Benziger Family Winery
Field Stone Winery

Foppiano Vineyards
Quivira Estate Vineyards & Winery
Sebastiani Vineyards & Winery
Trentadue Winery

WEDDING/EVENT FACILITIES
Benziger Family Winery
Buena Vista Winery
Chateau St. Jean
Chateau Souverain
Cline Cellars
Ferrari-Carano Vineyards & Winery
Korbel Champagne Cellars
Kunde Estate Winery & Vineyards
Rodney Strong Vineyards
  (meeting space)
St. Francis Winery & Vineyards
Sebastiani Vineyards & Winery
Simi Winery
Trentadue Winery

# Triangle Tours

One winery alone may be your destination, and there are plenty in this book that qualify with their tours, restaurants, picnic settings, wine and food programs, and events. If you are more ambitious and would like to fit in more than one, below are some "triangle tours." Three wineries are optimum for visiting in one day. Here I make suggestions for two or three that are close in geography, with ideas on how to visit and where to have lunch. Most of the wineries are within 20 minutes of each other. The shortest distance and the longest are in Western Sonoma. For the first triangle tour, two of the wineries are next to each other and the third is a quarter mile away. This gives you time to explore food and wine treats in Healdsburg. The longest tour is the last one, which covers a beautiful area of Sonoma from the Russian River through the redwoods to Green Valley. For this one begin either at Iron Horse or Hop Kiln and prepare for a glorious drive.

SOUTHERN SONOMA COUNTY

Cline Cellars/lunch at Viansa Winery & Italian Marketplace/Gloria Ferrer Champagne Caves tour

Ravenswood Winery tour (call ahead)/picnic at Buena Vista Winery or lunch in Sonoma/Sebastiani Vineyards historical and trolley tours

Kunde Estate Winery cave tour/lunch at Chateau St. Jean/St. Francis Winery Reserve Room tasting

Matanzas Creek Winery lavender walk/picnic and tram tour at Benziger Family Winery/visit Jack London State Park or Glen Ellen and the Olive Press

Buena Vista Winery historical tour/lunch in Sonoma or picnic at Gundlach-Bundschu Winery/Gundlach-Bundschu cave tour

NORTHERN SONOMA COUNTY

Seghesio Family Vineyards with bocce and picnic/or lunch in Healdsburg/Simi Winery tour

Field Stone Winery with picnic/or picnic at Alexander Valley Vineyards/Simi Winery tour

Trentadue Winery Port tasting/lunch at Chateau Souverain/Geyser Peak Winery reserve tasting

Dry Creek Vineyards or Quivira Winery tour (call ahead)/Preston of Dry Creek (all excellent picnic sites; pick up provisions at Dry Creek Store or in Healdsburg)

Ferrari-Carano Vineyard's garden walk/picnic at Fritz Winery or alfresco lunch at Chateau Souverain or Geyser Peak Winery

WESTERN SONOMA COUNTY

Foppiano Vineyards tour and picnic/J Vineyards & Winery bar or Bubble Room tasting/Rodney Strong Vineyards winery tour (3:00 P.M.) (If not picnicking, plan for lunch in Healdsburg)

Hop Kiln Winery/lunch at Korbel Champagne Cellars/Iron Horse Vineyards

# Wineries

# Southern
# Sonoma County

# Benziger Family Winery

Benziger Family Winery
1883 London Ranch Road
Glen Ellen, CA 95442
800-989-8890; 707-935-4046
Fax: 707-935-3016
Website: benziger.com
Email: greatwine@benziger.com

Winemakers: Mike Benziger, Joe
Benziger, Terry Noland
Winery owner: Benziger family

## Access
Location: About 1 mile from Glen
Ellen. From Sonoma take Napa
Street west to Arnold Drive, and turn
right; when you reach Glen Ellen,
turn left on London Ranch Road.
The winery is about 1 mile up on
the right.

Hours open for visits and tastings:
10:00 A.M. – 5:00 P.M. daily,
except major holidays.

## Tastings and Tours
Charge for tasting? Yes. $5 for vine-
yard designates; $10 for reserve,
estate, and biodynamic wines.

Appointment necessary for tour?
No, but recommended.

Tours: Complimentary self-guided
tours at Vineyard Discovery Center.
Vineyard Tram Tour, $10 for
45-minute tour (includes tasting),
11:00 A.M. – 3:30 P.M. daily. ☞

When the Benzigers moved from New York to the 85-acre parcel west of the tiny town of Glen Ellen, they knew location was important for successful grape growing. The property, which is on the way to Jack London's ranch on Sonoma Mountain, is situated in a bowl-shaped vale, with microclimates that nurture Sauvignon Blanc and Semillon as well as Merlot and Cabernet Sauvignon grapes. Eight soil types have been identified in this caldera of an ancient volcano, with steep sides that relax into a flat bottom. To the Benzigers, the narrow vineyard terraces, with their concentration of diverse grape-growing conditions, are like a spice rack of possibilities.

The Benzigers coined the phrase "farming for fla-vor" as a way to describe the fortunate circumstances of their property. And they've created an intensive Sonoma Mountain Estate Tour to show it off. But first, you may want to get acquainted with the grounds on your own.

Next to the parking lot is the Vineyard Discovery Center. Pick up the self-guided tour booklet and get ready to learn about many aspects of grape growing. Benziger is a bio-dynamically farmed ranch, which means not only does it forgo the use of pesticides in favor of organic cover crops and beneficial insects, but planting and composting are reg-ulated by natural rhythms. Take a walk to the Insectory, a "Club Med for Bugs," to experience biodiversity. Shiny-backed flies, fat yellow-and-black striped bees, and small wasps with big wings buzz and hover around various plantings on a verdant knoll that pops up as if this was its predestined use. Back at the Discovery Center, a display of bird boxes shows the preferred housing of barn owls, kestrels, and blue birds. A rootstock nursery, in-depth grafting exhibit, soil diorama, and vineyard calendar are designed to appeal to everyone from young children to the experienced oenophile.

The Sonoma Mountain Estate Tour is the most advanced viticulture tour in the industry. The motorized tour begins in front of the farmhouse. After an introduc-tion to the winery and a stop to look at the rootstock nursery, you'll be transported up the steep hill to the Parthenon for a short geology and biodynamic grape-growing lesson. At this and the other stops around the estate, you are encouraged to touch and compare the vines and soil and to ask questions. So much information is passed on, you'll be glad there isn't an exam at the end!

The grapes that grow best in these well-drained vol-canic soil vineyards are Bordeaux varieties such as Cabernet Sauvignon, Merlot, Malbec, Semillon, Sauvignon Blanc, and Cabernet Franc. In addition to the eight soil types, twenty-nine flavor blocks have been identified on the property. You'll learn that the Cabernet grown on the northwest-facing hill produces grapes that taste of cherry, while the Cabernet on the opposite hill develops a black-berry flavor.

Pruning and trellising styles are determined by the amount of sun exposure, the size of the leaves, and angles of the hill. The Sauvignon Blanc block you see on one stop grows so rigorously that it develops too many leaves, which can make the flavor extremely grassy and vegeta-tive. To tone that down the vines are trellised on a split

Typical wines offered: Fumé Blanc, Chardonnay, Muscat Canelli; Cabernet Sauvignon, Merlot, Petite Sirah, Pinot Noir, Syrah, Zinfandel; Port.

Sales of wine-related items? Yes, including shirts, books, dishes, glassware, and original art.

**Picnics and Programs**
Picnic area open to the public? Yes.

Picnic ingredients sold in Tasting Room? Yes, including Sonoma Jack cheese, Molinari salami, crackers, Benziger dipping sauces, and more.

Special events or wine-related programs? Pinot Passion in February; Heart of the Valley Barrel Tasting in March; Holiday Open House in November.

Wine Club: Imagery Club members receive pre-release wine shipments 7 times a year, discounts on wine and merchandise, personalized tour, waived tasting fees, and member-only events.

canopy, so more fruit is exposed. The goal is to open the fruit to sunlight and increase the quality and the crop load.

If you take the tour in the winter, you'll see the way vines are pruned. In the spring you can count the number of strings hand-tied on each cane to hold it to the trellis. In the summer you'll stand amid hot vines laden with voluptuous fruit and see how the various trellises work for each type of grape. At harvest you might even be invited to cut a cluster with the sharp, curved harvesting knife. In autumn, as the temperature changes and affects each of the microclimates, the vines reveal their differences in variety by hues, in sections of red, yellow, bronze, and gold.

After the hillside discussions, the next stop is the crushing and fermentation areas, which can be quite hectic during harvest. From here, it's a short walk to the 28,000 square feet of caves used for barrel storage. The tour finishes with a tasting in which you can sample the wines grown in different soils.

If this visit only makes you want more, a couple of miles away is the Benziger family's Imagery Estate Winery. Outside, you can meander along the "Appellation Trail" and learn about ten different grapes in the Varietal Display. Inside the tasting room is an art lovers' gallery full of the original paintings made for the labels of the Imagery's wines. When you inhale the wine's aroma in your glass, then hold a sip in your mouth, think of mint, pepper, clove, sage, cinnamon, and all the other herbaceous, fruity, and vegetal components extracted from grapes and see if you can taste them in your glass of wine. It's the best way to understand what "farming for flavors" is all about.

# Buena Vista Winery

**Buena Vista Winery**
18000 Old Winery Road
Sonoma, CA 95476
800-926-1266; 707-938-1266
Fax: 707-939-0916
Website: buenavistawinery.com
Email: bvw_info@buenavista
winery.com

Winemaker: Jeff Stewart
Winery owner: Allied Domecq
Wines USA

**Access**
Location: About 2½ miles northeast
of Sonoma. From Sonoma turn
east on East Napa Street, then turn
left on Old Winery Road, and follow it
to the end.

Hours open for visits and tastings:
10:00 A.M. – 5:00 P.M. daily,
except major holidays;
Buena Vista Sonoma Plaza Tasting
Room open 11:00 A.M. daily.

**Tastings and Tours**
Charge for tasting? Yes. $5 for 4
wines, includes souvenir glass; $10
for Library Collection tasting flight
of 3 wines; other wines such as Port
tastings as available.

Appointment necessary for tour? No,
but recommended in the summer.

Tours: Complimentary self-guided
tours any time. Guided 1½ hour
Historical Tour, $15, 11:00 A.M. &
2:00 P.M. daily.

As the oldest premium winery in Sonoma and one of the pioneers in the industry, Buena Vista holds a place of honor. After passing through the gates on Old Winery Road, you walk up the lane past a thicket of blackberries to the stone cellars, where it is cathedral-quiet. Whether because sound is absorbed in the giant eucalyptus trees or everyone speaks in hushed tones, a frog's croak from the creek and the occasional flit of a bird through branches are as loud as it gets.

Although the setting looks like it did a hundred years ago, many things have changed at Buena Vista. There's no winery here anymore, and that contributes to the hush. The wine is made at a huge state-of-the-art facility several miles south in Carneros, and Buena Vista's label now includes the Carneros appellation. The grapes grown on the original vineyards across the creek are made into wine for other wineries.

The winery setting is as beautiful as it was when Agoston Haraszthy planted his first grapes here more than 130 years ago. The present owner, Allied Domecq, takes its guardianship of Haraszthy's legacy seriously. You can take the self-guided tour, with its impressive photographic exhibits and glimpse into the old cellar, or take a guided tour. One, offered twice daily, is a historical tour that includes extra elaboration on the exhibits, a viticultural demonstration, and a sit-down tasting. The other, offered on Saturdays, is the Sonoma Wine & Cheese Experience, which focuses on the relationship of *terroir* to wine and cheese making using local artisan cheeses and Buena Vista wines.

Sonoma Experience, $50,
12:30 P.M. Saturday, includes
2-hour tour, guided tasting. Limited
seating.

Typical wines offered: Blanc de
Blancs sparkling wine; Chardonnay,
Sauvignon Blanc, Gewürztraminer;
Cabernet Sauvignon, Gamay
Beaujolais, Merlot, Pinot Noir; also
at times in tasting room only, old
Buena Vista specialties: Spiceling
and Lachryma Montis (a red blend).

Sales of wine-related items? Yes, an
emporium of food, picnic items,
crafts, and clothes.

**Picnics and Programs**
Picnic area open to the public? Yes.

Picnic ingredients sold in Tasting
Room? Yes, including cheese,
salami, crackers, bread, sodas,
and water.

Special events or wine-related programs? Check website for special
events at the tasting room. Holiday
in Carneros in December and April
in Carneros Open House at the
Carneros winery, 27000 Ramal
Road; 707-252-7117.

Wine Club: The Count's Wine Club
members receive customized wine
shipments and special discounts,
and are invited to members-only
luncheons and other events.

If you didn't bring a picnic, you can pick up all you need in the tasting room and settle in front of the stone cellars. Then immerse yourself in the story of California viticulture.

Agoston Haraszthy de Mokesa was born on August 30, 1812, in what is now Serbia, but then was part of the Kingdom of Hungary in the Austrian Empire. Before being exiled in 1842 for supporting independence, he served in the military and was a bureaucrat and grape grower.

After immigrating to America with his family, he found his way to Sonoma, where he soon met Sonoma legislator Mariano Vallejo. The two, both wine lovers, mutually recognized the area's potential. In 1857 Haraszthy purchased 560 acres east of Sonoma in the Mayacamas foothills. Convinced that European grapes were the means of success, Haraszthy made a trip to Europe, returning a year later with a hundred thousand cuttings, including Riesling, Flame Tokay, Traminer, and more. In his enthusiasm he encouraged European vintners to move to Sonoma, and helped instigate the first land boom in the area (prices shot from $6 to $150 an acre). He sent his sons to Europe to learn winemaking, built three stone caves, produced sixty-five hundred gallons of wine a year, and shipped excess grapes to San Francisco. In 1860 he released Eclipse, his first sparkling wine.

The idyll didn't last long. Never one to slow down, in 1869 Haraszthy went to Nicaragua to see about opening a brandy distillery. His horse was found tied to a tree with Haraszthy's footprints leading into a crocodile-infested river. He was never seen again.

Shortly after Haraszthy's departure, the first devastating attack of phylloxera took place, ruining most of Buena Vista's vineyards. Then in 1906 the San Francisco earthquake collapsed the caves here, destroying much of the wine. Prohibition was the final blow, and Buena Vista lay dormant until the 1940s, when it was sold at auction to United Press International journalist Frank Bartholomew and his wife Toni.

Within five years the Bartholomews had replanted the vineyards, reinforced the caves, and resurrected the winery. For the next two decades Buena Vista regained recognition with premium wines. In 1968 Bartholomew sold the winery. Buena Vista changed hands a couple of times, and additions included the acquisition of eight hundred acres in the Carneros.

Grapes grown on the Carneros estate include Cabernet Sauvignon, Pinot Noir, Merlot, Zinfandel, Chardonnay, and Gewürztraminer. Although the winery is open to the public only two weekends a year, the wines are available in the tasting room in Buena Vista's original press house. Three tiers of wines include Buena Vista Classics, Carneros Estate, and Carneros Grand Reserve Wine, with the focus on Chardonnay, Pinot Noir, and Merlot.

If you are interested in more history and would like to complement this visit, just outside Buena Vista's gate is the entrance to Bartholomew Memorial Park. The reproduction of Haraszthy's Pompeian villa and Bartholomew Park Winery, which opened in 1994 in one of the out buildings, are open to the public. Both the winery and the villa have excellent historical exhibitions on the people who owned this property and on the winemaking story of Sonoma. Visiting all three places is an excellent way to pay homage to the origins of California viticulture.

# Chateau St. Jean

Chateau St. Jean
8555 Sonoma Highway 12
P.O. Box 293
Kenwood, CA 95452
707-833-4134
Fax: 707-833-4200
Website: chateaustjean.com
Email: csjtr@chateaustjean.com

Winemaker: Margo Van Staaveren
Winery owner: Beringer Blass Wine Estates

**Access**
Location: About 10 miles from Sonoma and 10 miles from Santa Rosa. Just north of Kenwood on the east side of Highway 12.

Hours open for visits and tastings: 10:00 A.M. – 5:00 P.M. daily, except major holidays.

**Tastings and Tours**
Charge for tasting? Yes. Sampler of 5 wines, $5, applied to purchase. Reserve tasting in comfortable seating in the old Chateau, $10.

Appointment necessary for tour? No, but recommended.

Tours: Self-guided garden tours any time. Winery tours: $15, includes logo wine glass ($5 applied to wine purchase), 11:00 A.M. & 3:00 P.M. daily; Guided Wine Education.

Tastings: Private Tour & Tasting, $25; Come to Your Senses wine component tasting, $15 with minimum of 4 guests; Dynamics of Food & Wine, $25, minimum of 4 guests; Wine Blending workshop, $35, minimum of 4 guests.

Typical wines offered: Chardonnay, Fumé Blanc, Johannisberg Riesling, Gewürztraminer, Pinot Blanc, Cabernet Franc, Cabernet Sauvignon, Pinot Noir, Malbec, and Merlot.

Sales of wine-related items? Yes, including dishes, cutting boards, books, linens, wine racks, antiques, and more. ☞

The estate gardens and Mediterranean architecture of Chateau St. Jean present a beautiful backdrop for this leading California winery. Located at the foot of Sugarloaf Ridge, the property surrounding Chateau St. Jean was part of a 19,000-acre Mexican land grant in 1837. In 1849 William Hood planted the first grapes on the ranch he named Los Guilicos.

The 250 acres that are now Chateau St. Jean's passed from Hood to L. H. Sly in the 1860s and to Ernest and Maude Goff in 1916. The Goffs came with their four children from Saginaw, Michigan, and built the stately chateau-style home you see from the road. The architecture and grounds with fountains and statuary preserve the refinement of a bygone era, as do the winery buildings, built in 1975, and the visitor's center, added in 2000. This is a site to linger in, to learn about the flora, taste the wines, and enjoy a picnic from the fully stocked charcuterie in the visitor's center. If you call ahead, you can reserve a space in one of the excellent guided wine and culinary tastings or bring a group and create your own blend of red or white wine. The comprehensive winery tour takes you on an informational jaunt up to the top of the bell tower, with its bird's-eye view of the valley and mountains.

But first a little more history. In 1973, table grape growers from the San Joaquin Valley, Robert and Edward Merzoian and Kenneth Sheffield, purchased the property from the Goff estate and founded the winery. They named it after Edward's wife Jean (Kenneth's sister and Robert's sister-in-law). The graceful statue of Jean, modeled from a photograph in 1980, is a focal point in the garden.

Ninety-three acres of estate vineyards were planted, some on terraced blocks in the hills behind the winery. Varietals include Cabernet Sauvignon, Chardonnay, Johannisberg Riesling, Merlot, Cabernet Franc, Petite Verdot, and Malbec. Pinot Noir is grown for Chateau St. Jean in Carneros, Chardonnay in Alexander Valley, and Sauvignon Blanc in the Russian River Valley. Under the direction of the first winemaker, Dick Arrowood (who left in 1990 to start his own winery a few miles south of here), Chateau St. Jean pioneered the separation of vineyard lots, labeling certain wines by their vineyards. The winery was built to accommodate a multitude of small lots. In the barrel room, hundreds of barrels are labeled with their respective sources.

It was Chateau St. Jean's commitment to showcasing the best of their vineyards that led to their practice of keeping vineyard lots separate. In France, the term *terroir* refers to a site-specific combination of soil, climate, and growing conditions. This is what makes wines consistently distinctive and recognizable. Two examples that have become synonymous with this quality concept are the Chardonnay wines made from Robert Young Vineyard and Belle Terre Vineyard, both in Alexander Valley.

You can find out for yourself what the difference is when you taste them. Compare Chardonnays from the Robert Young and Belle Terre vineyards and see if one is fruitier or drier, if one tastes buttery, the other like apples and honeysuckle, or if you can detect any oakiness. The knowledgeable staff is a great resource to help define the nuances found in any of their varietals. They want you to learn something while you are here, which is why Chateau St. Jean offers so many types of guided tastings—to further educate the public and demystify wine and its combination with food.

Save time to meander the courtyards and flower gardens around the visitor's center and the chateau. The Goffs counted Luther Burbank as a friend, which is probably why the gardens got off to a good start. Pick up a map, which identifies many of the plants, from Chinese lanterns to Japanese aralia, Dalmatian bellflower to pink clematis. Many plants are labeled. The grandiose stretch of lawn to the west, the formal gardens, the demonstration vineyard, and the tables in the tasting terrace contribute to the romance of this beautiful setting, a place to immerse yourself in architectural and horticultural glories.

### Picnics and Programs

Picnic area open to the public? Yes.

Picnic ingredients sold in Tasting Room? Yes, charcuterie-style deli completely stocked with meats, pâtés, cheeses, salads, bread, and more.

Special events or wine-related programs? Heart of the Valley Barrel Tasting in March; Fete des Fleurs wine release party in May; Open House events on Memorial Day, Labor Day, and Thanksgiving weekends; Festival of the Lights in December. Event and wedding facilities.

Wine Club: Club St. Jean offers quarterly wine shipments, discounts on wine and merchandise, complimentary wine tasting for 4, and member-only events.

# Cline Cellars

Cline Cellars
24737 Highway 121
Sonoma, CA 95476
800-546-2070; 707-940-4030
Fax: 707-935-4319
Website: clinecellars.com
Email: See website for list of options

Winemaker: Charlie Tsegeletos
Winery owners: Fred and Nancy
Cline

**Access**
Location: About 6 miles south of
Sonoma. From Highway 101 take
Highway 37 east, then take
Highway 121 (Arnold Drive); go
north 4½ miles and turn left at the
entrance.

Hours open for visits and tastings:
10:00 A.M. – 6:00 P.M. daily,
except Thanksgiving and
Christmas.

**Tastings and Tours**
Charge for tasting? No, except
nominal fee for reserve tasting.

Appointment necessary for tour?
No, but recommended in winter.

Tours: 11:00 A.M., 1:00 P.M. &
3:00 P.M. daily, no charge.

Typical wines offered: Pinot
Gris/Chardonnay; Marsanne,
Viognier; Rosé; Carignane,
Cinsault, Merlot, Mourvèdre,
Syrah, Zinfandel; plus other labels
including Jacuzzi and Red Truck.

Sales of wine-related items? Yes,
including books, dishes, and linens.

**Picnics and Programs**
Picnic area open to the public? Yes.

Picnic ingredients sold in Tasting
Room? Yes, including Sonoma Jack
cheese, salami, chips, sodas,
baguettes, Cline olives, dressings,
chocolate, and other Sonoma food
items. Fresh bread delivered 3
times a week.

Special events or wine-related programs? Winemaker dinners at the
winery; April in Carneros; Easter
Sunrise Service; ☞

In the heart of the Carneros, Fred Cline and his wife Nancy are stewarding one of southern Sonoma's treasures. Once the site of a Miwok village and later the first temporary Mission San Francisco de Solano, this is a winery where you can enjoy a picnic and a whole afternoon. You can also have a wedding or other event here.

The most beguiling feature of the winery, site of the former Rancheria Pulpuli, which was part of the Mexican land grant of Petaluma, is its six spring-fed ponds. Established in the 1880s by Mr. J. A. Poppe, these are the oldest farm-raised carp ponds in California. Carp still flash their golden sides, but are raised strictly for pleasure these days. Mr. Poppe imported the original carp from his native Germany and sold them for a dollar a pound in 1882. Children love to see both the fish and the old turtles that bask lazily on floating logs (except in winter, when they hibernate).

You are welcome to wander along the paths around the ponds, bath house, and "mission," or you can take a guided tour of the winemaking facilities from crush pad to bottling room. The old bath house straddles one of the streams. A Plexiglas window covers the door now, but you can imagine the menthol aroma of eucalyptus berries scenting the steamy air from the natural warm spring that feeds the built-in tub. The water bubbles out of a waterfall at the top of the nearby pond. The time-honored tradition of carving initials in wood is upheld in the bath house walls. See if you can find a date earlier than J. W. Robb's in 1877.

The "mission" is what the Clines call the building with the bell tower. It is made of old adobe bricks and is used as an entertainment venue. Continuing your walk around the back of the farm-style tasting room brings you to the large birdcages, featuring exotic quail and pheasant. Cards on the cages give a little information on each. The Mission Discovery Center houses models of the original Sonoma mission, which were made for the 1939 World Fair on Treasure Island.

Across the road is the winery. At harvest time trucks roll in loaded with Zinfandel, Mourvèdre, and Carignane grapes grown at the Cline family's vineyards in Oakley. The success of the Clines, who have built a ster-ling reputation for their Rhône-style grapes and wine, is due to salesmanship, luck, and discernment.

Fred Cline is the oldest of nine children and the grandson of Valeriano Jacuzzi, the inventor of the pump spa. Grandpa Jacuzzi settled in the Sacramento Delta and planted three hundred acres of grapes in Oakley a hundred years ago. When he died, Fred, who was raised in Los Angeles, moved to the ranch to help his grandmother and earn his viticulture degree at the University of California at Davis. In 1982 he used his small inheritance to establish a winery. Since he was not on a route that lures a steady stream of visitors, he looked to the Carneros and was able to purchase this foreclosed 300-acre ranch at a bargain in 1989. The Clines built the winery in 1991. They are also responsible for the Jacuzzi wine label and its planned premises across the highway.

Many of the grapes for the 250,000 cases of Cline wines come from the Oakley ranch in Contra Costa County. On a clear day you can see Mount Diablo from the vineyard, as well as from their Oakley property. When he purchased the Carneros land, Fred planted the Carneros-loving Chardonnay and Pinot Noir along with Rhône varieties such as Marsanne, Viognier, Alicante Bouschet, and Syrah. These plus Carignane and Mourvèdre are among the varietals that grow in the 125-

Holiday in Carneros in December. Outdoor lawn area and indoor arena available for weddings and other catered events for up to 1,000 people.

Wine Club: Pendulum Club includes quarterly wine shipments, discount on wines, Rhône-style focus, exclusive tastings, free reserve tastings and special events. Full Swing Club receives the above plus full case shipments.

mile region along the Rhône River in southern France. The grapes produce mostly red, affordable wines that are meant to be drunk young, but also can be aged. In 1991, Fred, along with other producers of these wines, formed a loose-knit group of self-proclaimed "Rhône Rangers" to promote them. The Rhône Rangers hold a popular consumer tasting each year in San Francisco.

Around the encircling porch of the 1850s farmhouse tasting room as well as everywhere you look, roses bloom eight months of the year. Over two hundred varieties are included in the five thousand roses planted on the property. Ask the staff about the roses, a popular planting around vineyards in both France and California. You'll learn that they are practical as well as beautiful. According to popular wisdom, in a damp climate roses tend to mildew before grapes, thus making them valuable for identifying diseases before they strike the vines. As for beauty, roses have the most blossoms per square inch of any landscape plant and they bloom from March until October.

The well-trained staff inside the tasting room will help you increase your knowledge of wine. Cline's hearty reds are aged in French oak for over a year, which adds to their "dusty berry" flavors and aromas. Bring in some popcorn from the machine on the front porch and try it with Cline's wines. Whether you sip the wine, smell the roses, or walk on historical ground, this is a magical spot.

# Gloria Ferrer Champagne Caves

A Spanish cultural revival came to Sonoma in 1986 when Gloria Ferrer Champagne Caves opened in Carneros. The Ferrer family's emphasis on their heritage is evident in the winery's architecture, hospitality, and schedule of events.

In the 1600s, when their fellow countrymen were exploring the new territory that was to become California, Gloria Ferrer's parent company, Freixenet (pronounced *fresh-e-net*) had already been making wine for three hundred years in Sant Sadurní d'Anoia, a Catalonian town near Barcelona. Still a family-run company, Freixenet is the world's largest producer of *méthode champenoise* sparkling wine. José Ferrer, who heads the Freixenet companies, including wineries in Spain, France, Australia, and Mexico, named his Sonoma cellars after his wife and partner.

Amid the vineyards, the winery resembles a Spanish monastery on a California hill. Red barrel roof tiles, creamy adobe walls, and intricate wrought iron and woodwork throughout establish the ancestry of the design. A philosophy runs in the family that says, "It's important that we bring our Spanish heritage with us, no matter where we go in the world."

As you climb the stairs and walk along the porch you may feel a pervading aura of sanctity and even half-expect brown-frocked padres to pass in prayer. Any too-solemn thoughts in this beautiful cloister, however, tend to quickly reorient in the lively tasting room. Alongside the serious business of winemaking, the hospitality staff work full time putting on programs and celebrations, mostly with a Spanish emphasis.

In January, *El Dia de Los Reyes Magos*, the Feast of the Kings, is celebrated on the first Sunday of the year. It's a Spanish version of Twelfth Night, when according to Spanish lore the three kings, while paying homage to the Christ child, came from the East to Spain. At Gloria Ferrer the feast is commemorated with a procession of richly attired kings and a choral performance. This family event includes hot chocolate for the children, sparkling wine for the adults, and Spanish pastries for everyone.

A Catalan Festival of Food, Wine, and Music is celebrated in the summer. The yearly schedule continues with luncheons, Valentine's Day, a Mother's Day brunch, and a

daily agenda that includes tastings and tours of the winery. Appetizer seminars are available by appointment.

The tour includes an unforgettable visit through the 14,500 square feet of caves. It begins on the porch, where the guide explains that the low roof and thick archways typically surrounding Spanish buildings are designed as a cooling buffer against summer heat.

At the nearby crush pad the presses are used to extract juice from Chardonnay and Pinot Noir grapes. The gentle pressing of small lots is a typical *méthode champenoise* technique. Typically grapes for sparkling wine are among the first picked in the season because the first grapes have less sugar and higher acid, both of which are desirable for making premium sparkling wine. Here you learn that

**Gloria Ferrer Champagne Caves**
23555 Highway 121 (also Carneros Highway)
P.O. Box 1427
Sonoma, CA 95476
707-996-7256
Fax: 707-996-0720
Website: gloriaferrer.com
Email: information@gloriaferrer.com

Winemaker: Bob Iantosca
Winery owner: Freixenet S.A., Sant Sadurní d'Anoia, Catalonia, Spain

**Access**
Location: About 5 miles south of Sonoma on Highway 121 (Carneros Highway). From Highway 101 take Highway 37 east to Highway 121 north. Winery is in about 5 miles, on the left.

Hours open for visits and tastings: 10:30 A.M. – 5:30 P.M. daily, except major holidays.

**Tastings and Tours**
Charge for tasting? Yes. Sparkling wines $4 – $7.50; still wines $2 – $3. Flights when available; price varies.

Appointment necessary for tour? No, but recommended.

Tours: Complimentary. Noon, 2:00 P.M. & 4:00 P.M. daily.

Typical wines offered: Brut, Blanc de Noirs, Blanc de Blancs, Brut Rosé, and other cuvées of sparkling ☞

wines; Chardonnay; Pinot Noir, Merlot, Syrah.

Sales of wine-related items? Yes, including glassware, books, and logo clothing.

**Picnics and Programs**
Picnic area open to the public? Yes.

Picnic ingredients sold in Tasting Room? Yes, including Spanish cheeses, tapas, salami, olives, and more.

Special events or wine-related programs? Appetizer seminars by appointment. Many events, especially with Catalan focus including Catalan Festival of Food, Wine, and Music in the summer; holiday season Catalan luncheon; Three Kings Day children's event; Mother's Day Brunch, Valentine's Day with Chocolate.

Wine Club: The Cuvée Club offers quarterly shipments, discounts on wine, merchandise, winery events, facility rental for private events, and more.

the hang time is a little longer than usual, giving a richer dimension and texture to Gloria Ferrer's sparkling wines.

Realizing the bounty of their location, Gloria Ferrer is also bottling the estate-grown Chardonnay and Pinot Noir, plus Syrah and Merlot as varietals. In the tasting room, flights of sparkling and still wines are offered to encourage you to compare and contrast Chardonnay with and without bubbles, and Pinot Noir from sparkling to Regular vintage to reserve.

Inside the winery, a visitor's room overlooks the bottling and disgorging line. Then you make the descent into a 100-foot-long cave, where the initial ambience of hallowedness resumes. This time it is evoked by dim light and the glint of a hundred thousand bottles. In the background you may be treated to the rhythmic *dut-dut* of an invisible riddler, reverberating like a solo Gregorian chant. An eighth of a turn, an eighth of a turn—6,250 bottles an hour every day for four to five weeks. One-fourth of the wine here is riddled by hand. The rest is machine riddled,

which takes less than one week. Before ascending the stairway, look out over the grand arched cave, where each bottle spends two and a half to five years developing bubbles and flavor. It's too bad the wine can't appreciate the ethereal beauty of the surrounding chamber.

If you've packed a picnic, a spectacular place to feast is outside the tasting room on the veranda. The view encompasses the whole of the Carneros, extending from the fertile, sandy vineyards below to Mount Diablo in the southeast, the entrance to Napa Valley to the east, and Sonoma Mountain to the north. It is also a perfect place for watching bird migrations.

Before you depart, a Catalan toast may be offered when one of the staff raises a glass and says with typical Ferrer hospitality, *Salut! I que per molts anys puguem disfrutar-la!* To our health! And many years to be able to enjoy it!

# Gundlach-Bundschu Winery

Gundlach-Bundschu Winery
2000 Denmark Street
Sonoma, CA 95476
707-938-5277
Fax: 707-938-9460
Website: gunbun.com
Email: info@gunbun.com

Winemaker: Linda Trotta
Winery owners: Jim Bundschu and
Jeff Bundschu

**Access**
Location: About 2 miles southeast
of Sonoma. From Sonoma take
Napa Road East and turn right on
Eighth Street East. Turn left at
Denmark and continue around the
sharp right angle. The driveway is
on the left.

Hours open for visits and tastings:
11:00 A.M. – 4:30 P.M. daily,
except major holidays.

**Tastings and Tours**
Charge for tasting? Yes. $5 for the
daily selection.

Appointment necessary for tour?
Not on weekends; yes on weekdays.
Tour: Cave Tour on weekends on the
hour beginning at noon.

Typical wines offered: Chardonnay,
Gewürztraminer; Cabernet Franc,
Cabernet Sauvignon, Merlot, Pinot
Noir, Zinfandel; Bearitage blend.

Sales of wine-related items? Yes,
including shirts, logo glasses, and
copies of the posters.

The four hundred acres of Gundlach-Bundschu's Rhinefarm extend from the Mayacamas foothills like a big welcome mat. In the summer clusters of poppies line the one-lane driveway that extends between vineyard rows. Directly ahead is the family's Rhine-style house, a lovingly kept vestige of the property's history. If you think this visit to one of California's oldest vineyards will be a sentimental journey into the past, as you turn left and head up the hill, you are in for a surprise.

Those familiar with Gundlach-Bundschu's playful advertising posters know that the interplay of old and new, of wit and audacity, come with the territory. The first of these is exemplified by a vibrant contemporary mural at the back of the 130-year-old stone cellar. Painted by San Francisco muralists Eduardo Peneda and Ray Patlan, the scenes celebrate the Mexican American contributions to California winemaking. The mural covers a 120-foot wall in front of the fermenting tanks. Recognizable faces include retired vineyard manager Marcello Hernandez, owner Jim Bundschu, and retired general manager Lance Cutler. In the last panel are founders Jacob Gundlach and Charles Bundschu, barbecuing a few wursts for a harvest party. Vignettes from the mural have been reproduced as labels for reserve wines.

Around the corner, the lichen-covered stone building and an old mission bell effect a nostalgic façade. A plaque over the door establishes bonded winery number 64 as the sixty-fourth winery in California to receive its operating license. Inside, a hodgepodge of memorabilia, awards, and the posters that continue to attract attention, crammed into the seemingly always busy tasting room. Usually a wild and rhythmic CD is playing contemporary rock, jazz, or blues. On the walls are copies of the poster ads, which are known for playing on Gundlach-Bundschu's name or parodying drinking. At the bar, on a cave tour, or from a brochure you can learn the winery's story.

In 1858 Jim's great-great-grandfather, Jacob Gundlach, who immigrated to San Francisco in 1850, and fellow German Rhinelander Emil Dresel bought this acreage. They began planting grapes, at the time mostly Riesling, which is now a historical footnote. In 1875 Gundlach brought in Charles Bundschu, his future son-in-law, as a partner, and they made and bottled Bacchus Wines. Schooners came up Sonoma Creek at high tide, picked up the wine in barrels, and took it to be aged and bottled at the warehouse in San Francisco, where the two families lived.

Everything went along well until 1906, when the earthquake and fire demolished the warehouse and all the inventory. The Gundlach and Bundschu families moved to the Rhinefarm, where they made wine until Prohibition. Then, for the next sixty years, the family concentrated on farming. They added cattle and pears to the vineyards and sold grapes to Inglenook, Martini, and Sebastiani over the years.

The return to winemaking came in the late 1960s when Jim Bundschu talked his father, Towle, into converting the whole ranch back to wine grapes. At the time the old stone winery had only three walls remaining, and it had to be rebuilt. By 1973, Gundlach-Bundschu Winery was reestablished and produced six hundred cases. Now production is up to forty-five thousand cases, and fifteen different wines are made from grapes grown on the farm.

To accommodate so many wines, the bottling line, right inside the front door of the tasting room, could be rattling along any time you visit. An air of humor keeps everything light and fun, especially when Jim Bundschu's Sonoma Wine Patrol perpetrates another escapade. His raiders have been known to invade the Napa Wine Train and run through the cars pouring Sonoma wines. They've

**Picnics and Programs**

Picnic area open to the public? Yes.

Picnic ingredients sold in Tasting Room? Yes, including Vella cheese, prosciutto, pâté, crackers, and bread on weekends.

Special events or wine-related programs? Shakespeare, Mozart, and movie screenings in summer (bring picnic, chair, sunglasses; and blanket). Many more events; check the website.

Wine Club: Wine of the Moment Club members receive wine shipments, special discounts, notices of new and library wine releases, and an invitation to the Harvest Party and Holiday Toy Drive.

also hijacked a bus of travel writers in Napa and diverted it to Sonoma. Jim's son, Jeff, is also on the job, bringing the next generation's wit and irreverence. He is one of the founders of the Wine Brats, an irreverent organization dedicated to demystifying wine with events around the country.

Directly across from the tasting room is the ten-thousand-square-foot subterranean cave for barrel storage and aging that was completed in 1991. Windows on the doors allow you to see down the gunnite-covered tunnel to an aisle of some of the eighteen hundred French and American oak barrels inside. On a tour you'll learn that the ambient temperature remains at 60°F and the humidity keeps evaporation at around 2 percent, making the cave cost-effective for storing wine. Barrels, half made in France and half in America, are used for only five years. Chardonnay spends up to six months in oak and the red wines between twelve and fourteen months.

Everyone brings a glass along on the tasting, and when the tour group steps out the other side of the cave, they can toast the magnificent view.

For an unguided superb angle on Sonoma Valley, take the "short, strenuous hike" up over the caves to the top of the hill. The trail is quite steep, so wear comfortable shoes, and watch out for poison oak. On any weekend, the grounds around the winery feel like a community park. Picnickers are everywhere—hiking, lounging on the hillsides, or sitting next to the pond. On summer evenings, Shakespeare and other theatrical events are performed, and movies are shown in the natural amphitheater.

The spirit of hospitality here is as generous as the business of making the wine is serious. An uncompromising boldness, especially in the highly rated red wines, is a tangible reflection of the style that has evolved through seven generations of Gundlachs and Bundschus, punctuated with an indispensable sense of humor.

# Kunde Estate Winery & Vineyards

Kunde Estate Winery & Vineyards
10155 Sonoma Highway 12
P.O. Box 639
Kenwood, CA 95452
707-833-5501
Fax: 707-833-2204
Website: kunde.com
Email: wineinfo@kunde.com

Winemaker: David Noyes
Winery owner: Kunde family

Access
Location: About 10 miles from
Sonoma and 10 miles from Santa
Rosa. On the east side of Sonoma
Highway 12.

Hours open for visits and tastings:
10:30 A.M. – 4:30 P.M. daily,
except major holidays.

Tastings and Tours
Charge for tasting? Yes. $5 for
4 estate wines, applied to purchase;
for reserve wines, $10 includes
Kunde Estate crystal logo glass.

Appointment necessary for tour?
Not on weekends. Yes,
Monday – Thursday.

Tours: Complimentary cave tours
Friday, Saturday & Sunday on the
hour, 11:00 A.M. – 3:00 P.M.

Typical wines offered: Chardonnay,
Sauvignon Blanc, Viognier;
Cabernet Sauvignon, Merlot, ☞

In the 1980s, the emphasis on winemaking in California changed from what the winemaker could do to bring out, balance, and add to the flavors of grapes to what is going on in the vineyards. Vintners realized the best wines are those that showcase fruit rather than oak or yeast. Flavor became more important than quantity.

While this was happening, one of Sonoma's oldest grape-growing families looked around their two-thousand-acre estate and decided it was time to take advantage of all the attention paid to fruit like theirs and make wine under their own label. After all, their grapes went into many of Sonoma's finest wines. Their relatives had made wine from 1904 to the 1940s. And the original picturesque stone winery, California bonded number 202, remained on the property. What really cinched the move was the decision of a number of family members to get involved.

Eight members of the extended Kunde family take part in daily operations, from vineyard management to marketing. They are one of the nicest groups of people you'll ever meet, which is one reason a visit is so enjoyable. Kunde's story continues in the vineyards with the soil, which is primarily volcanic red ash. On a Chardonnay-covered hillock next to the crush pad, the soil is littered with rocks of pumice, a porous stone that allows excellent drainage. These are left over from extinct volcanoes visible along the Mayacamas range on the eastern border of the property.

Syrah, Zinfandel; and small lots of estate varietals in the tasting room only.

Sales of wine-related items? Yes, including linens, dishes, books, and logo clothing.

**Picnics and Programs**
Picnic area open to the public? Yes.

Picnic ingredients sold in Tasting Room? Yes, including chips, salsa, condiments, sauces, chocolates, and estate olive oil.

Special events or wine-related programs? Heart of the Valley Barrel Tasting in March; Holiday Open House in November. Other events on website.

Wine Club: Cave Club members receive shipments of special and pre-release wines, discounts, and invitations to private events.

Eight hundred acres of vineyards allow Kunde's winemaker to be especially choosy. Numerous vineyard blocks and seven microclimates allow the winery to grow a wide variety of grapes including Chardonnay, Sauvignon Blanc, Semillon, Symphony, Viognier, Barbera, Cabernet Sauvignon, Carignane, Malbec, Merlot, Petite Sirah, Petite Verdot, and Zinfandel. As the grapes ripen, the winemaker goes up and down the rows, tasting, testing, and choosing which rows will be harvested for the estate.

Some of the blocks are named, preserving a historical chronology of the ranch. Drummond is the planting site of the Cabernet Sauvignon cuttings that the first owner, James Drummond, procured in 1879 from Chateau Margaux and Lafitte Rothschild, two of Bordeaux's most prestigious chateaux. Shaw Vineyard was planted in 1882, and twenty-eight of its acres still contain the original Zinfandel vines and the source for Kunde's Century Vines Zinfandel.

These vineyards became Kunde property after Louis Kunde emigrated from Germany in 1884. In 1904 he bought Wildwood Vineyards, established the winery, and began making wine. After he died, in 1922, his son Arthur (Big Boy) kept the winery going through Prohibition, but closed it when his sons went off to World War II. When they returned they concentrated on cattle raising until the 1960s, when the sons, Bob and Fred (who passed away in 1993) expanded the acreage to its present size and planted hundreds of acres of prime varietals. Then came the decision to build a winery. Although the tasting room and winery were finished in 1991, the building is an exact replica of the historic barn, which has been a fixture on the east side of Sonoma Highway near Kenwood since the 1800s.

Part of the construction included a system of caves carved into the hill under the Chardonnay vines. A tour of the caves, offered on the weekends, is worthwhile. As you pass through the beautiful doors and stone-lined entrance, you'll find a spelunker's delight: thirty-two thousand feet of tunnels holding five to six thousand American and French oak barrels. This isn't a set for Dungeons & Dragons, but it does feel magically gothic in the gray shotcrete-covered archways, where the only sounds are those of wine being racked and barrels being cleaned. At the

far end of the first tunnel, stairs leading up to an altar-like landing are lit by bead lights strung under each riser. This is where the Kundes host special events, 160 feet below the Chardonnay vines. An exposed wall shows the hill's treasures in a colorful collage of iron, pumice, granite, and other geologic elements. The tables and chairs in the dining area were built from the timbers of the original barn.

In the tasting room, where you can sample the wines, windows behind the bar give views of the bottling line and fermentation rooms. The designation "estate" was never more appropriate than at Kunde. You'll see that designation on all of Kunde's wines, which are made only from grapes grown on this property.

# Matanzas Creek Winery

**Matanzas Creek Winery**
6097 Bennett Valley Road
Santa Rosa, CA 95404
800-590-6464; 707-528-6464
Fax: 707-571-0156
Website: matanzascreek.com
Email: info@matanzascreek.com

Winemaker: Gary Patzwald
Winery owners: Jess Jackson and
Barbara Banke

### Access
Location: Between Sonoma Valley and Santa Rosa, in Bennett Valley. From Highway 101 north- or southbound take Highway 12 (Sonoma off-ramp) and stay in the right lane until you come to the stoplight. Turn right and continue to Bennett Valley Road. Winery is about 5 miles from the freeway on the left.

Hours open for visits and tastings: 10:00 A.M. – 4:30 P.M. daily, except major holidays.

### Tastings and Tours
Charge for tasting? Yes. $5 for selected flights.

Appointment necessary for tour? Yes.

Tours: By appointment, Monday – Friday 10:30 A.M. & 3:00 P.M.; weekends: 10:30 A.M. (maximum of 10 on a tour).

Typical wines offered: Chardonnay, Sauvignon Blanc; Cabernet Sauvignon, Merlot, Syrah.

Sales of wine-related items? Yes, including lavender bouquets, lotions, wands, and toiletries, logo glasses, clothing, Japanese teapots, and other tasteful items.

### Picnics and Programs
Picnic area open to the public? Yes, with purchase of wine.

Picnic ingredients sold in Tasting Room? No.

Special events or wine-related programs? Lavender Harvest Festival last Saturday in June. 🖝

Beginning in June at Matanzas Creek Winery, the blooms of five thousand French lavender plants scent the air with a heady perfume. The rest of the year, the silvery spiked tufts present three acres of texture against a palette of native and aromatic plantings. Inside the tasting room, there is also a hint of lavender, but not so much that it overpowers the taste of the wines.

The gardens and zenlike winery, created by founders Sandra and Bill McIver, provide a tasteful setting for the equally tasteful Bordeaux-style and other wines produced here. Matanzas Creek is located in the bucolic Bennett Valley, where cattle still roam, and where the Grange Hall, built in 1873, is the oldest in the United States. Bennett Valley Road, one of the most serene lanes in the county, connects Santa Rosa, just ten minutes away, with Sonoma Valley to the east.

Heading up the narrow straight driveway you'll have to go slowly and pull over for oncoming cars. A massive redwood fountain, sculpted by Bruce Johnson of Santa Rosa, marks the right turn to the winery.

Taking a self-guided tour of the gardens, created by Mendocino Coast master gardener Gary Ratway, allows immersion into the grounds, a compelling backdrop for this prestigious winery. Purchase a brochure in the tasting room (the information on the plants is worth the small charge) and you're on your way to six themed gardens, each a little different and yet all harmoniously connected. The tour takes you from the small shade garden with its brightly colored climbing hydrangea to the water garden, the courtyard garden, down the pathway garden, and into the lavender field.

Two cultivars of lavender grow here. Grosso is the dark blue variety, used mainly for oil, and Provençal is the most aromatic. As soon as the bottom flower opens, between mid-June and July, the lavender is harvested and hung upside down in the hay barn to dry. Bouquets are sold in the tasting room along with a variety of lavender-scented sachets, pillows, wands, and toiletries, as well as aromatherapy and culinary products, all made here.

Aesthetic details are evident throughout the winery. From the entrance terrace, be sure to notice the ingenious downspout that looks like a huge chain hanging from the roof. Inspired by a Japanese design, the winery's architect, Paul Hamilton, incorporated this system as an attractive way to direct the almost daily drip of condensation from the roof.

Inside the tasting room, you can stroll down the hallway to check out a display of winery photos and memorabilia, plus maps of the area. An infrared photograph measures the contour of vines in the ever-constant vigil for phylloxera damage. Infrared shots are taken from airplanes each year as a means of singling out a color or contour change that could point to the little louse's destructive arrival. Photographs of the former owners as well as the

Wine Club: Journey Society offers 3 tiers: Cellar, Barrel, and Estate. Each includes personalized shipments and priority access to limited-release and reserve wines, plus advance notice of winery dinners and tastings.

current owners, Jess Jackson and Barbara Banke, look over a display of grape vines under glass showing a cross section of roots and soils.

At the far end of the hallway, a window opens to the laboratory, where the winemaker or assistant can often be seen sampling and testing. One piece of equipment is a countertop spectrophotometer. This $10,000 instrument measures minute variations in color in the wine. The wine-maker can follow a wine's progress by using it over a period of time to check for browning, which would mean the wine is oxidizing.

Another window at the end of the hallway allows a view of the crush pad. From September through October trucks pull up and unload the grapes, beginning the process for the wines like those you are about to taste. You can call ahead anytime to take a more complete tour of the winery.

Back in the tasting room, a sunbeam from the round window above spotlights the Boton floor, a warm reminder of the gardens. While sampling current releases of Sauvignon Blanc, Chardonnay, Merlot, Cabernet Sauvignon, or Syrah, if you're curious about the winery's name, the story is worth requesting. In brief, a band of local Pomo Indians used to dress their deer in the creek that flows through the valley. When the Spanish came, they took the Spanish word *matanza*, which means slaughter, as the creek's name. With a glint in his eye, your server will finish the story with the question, "Does this mean Matanzas Creek wine is to die for?" As an expression, maybe, but with the winery's beautiful setting, gardens, and zenlike tasting room, the opposite is true.

# Ravenswood Winery

Ravenswood Winery
18701 Gehricke Road
Sonoma, CA 95476
888-669-4679; 707-933-2332
Fax: 707-938-9459
Website: ravenswood-wine.com
Email: rwwine@ravenswood-wine.com

Winemaker: Joel Peterson
Winery owner: Franciscan Estates

## Access

Location: About 1½ miles northeast of Sonoma. From the Plaza take East Napa Street or East Spain Street and turn left on Fourth Street East. Turn right on Lovall Valley Road and left on Gehricke Road; bear right at the fork and follow the signs to the parking lot.

Hours open for visits and tastings: 10:00 A.M. – 5:00 P.M. daily, except major holidays.

## Tastings and Tours

Charge for tasting? Yes. $5 for 5 wines, applied to purchase; $10 for 5 single vineyard designates, $5 applied to purchase.

Appointment necessary for tour? Yes.

Tours: $5, 10:30 A.M. daily; reservations required.

Typical wines offered: Chardonnay; Cabernet Franc, Cabernet Sauvignon, Merlot, Petite Sirah, Zinfandel; ICON (Rhône-style blend), Bordeaux-style blends, and other reds.

Sales of wine-related items? Yes, including books, shirts, and posters.

## Picnics and Programs

Picnic area open to the public? Yes.

Picnic ingredients sold in Tasting Room? No, but in the town of Sonoma are Vella Cheese Company, Sonoma Cheese Factory, and several other places to pick up ingredients. ☞

Few wineries in the world approach mecca status among their devotees. Ravenswood has that appeal to lovers of Zinfandel. In the charming hillside tasting room outside of Sonoma, you'll meet people from all over the country. Some are on a pilgrimage to taste their favorite Zin at the source. Some are on the grand winery tour. And others have come specifically to see if being here in person will raise their chances of getting a few more bottles from the limited allocations of their favorite vineyard designation.

The mystique of this peppery, berrylike, and sometimes rough-flavored dark red wine begins with the origins of the grape itself. After many years of speculation, the Zinfandel DNA has been found to match that of a grape indigenous to Croatia, as well as the Primitivo grape from Italy. For practical purposes, however, Zinfandel has grown in the state for close to 150 years, and by this name it is California's adopted wine grape.

Ravenswood's history begins in 1976, when winemaker and co-owner Joel Peterson contracted for a batch of Zinfandel grapes and rented a space to make them into wine at the late Joseph Swan's winery in the Russian River area. The recounting of his first experience, which produced three hundred cases of Zinfandel, is also the story of the winery's name and the significance of the ravens in the name and on the label.

As harvest time was nearing and rain was threatening, Joel had to decide whether to wait for a little more ripeness and chance the rain or to pick right away. Finally, he made the decision to pick. In the late afternoon, with menacing clouds looming overhead, Joel arrived at the vineyard to find that all the grapes had been picked and neatly stacked in bins at the ends of the rows and the crew had gone home.

Alone, Joel raced against the rain and loaded every bin onto the truck. As he worked in the waning light, three noisy ravens watched from the bleak silhouette of a tree, and Joel tried to remember whether ravens were a good sign or an omen of foreboding. By three o'clock in the morning he was pounding at Swan's door, and hours later the two of them had the grapes fermenting in open-top barrels. While they worked, Joel considered the ravens, and, an opera lover, he remembered the scene from *Lucia di Lammermoor* where Lord Ravenswood sinks to his death in quicksand—exactly how a new winemaker might feel upon entering the business. Ravenswood was named.

For the next fifteen years, Ravenswood wines were made in a shed on the edge of the Sangiacamo Ranch near Carneros. By 1978, Cabernet Sauvignon and Merlot had been added to Ravenswood's varietals.

In 1991, when the winery here on Gehricke Road became available, Ravenswood moved in. With the property came eighteen acres of vineyards. Three acres of Merlot are the block you see adjacent to the parking lot. Fifteen acres of Chardonnay on the hillside determined that Joel would apply his particular style to that grape as well. Thus, the motto "No Wimpy Wines" applies to all four hundred thousand cases of Ravenswood wines.

You have to reserve in advance to take the daily 10:30 A.M. tour of the winery, which is bound to enrich

RAVENS
WOOD

ZINFANDEL
SONOMA COUNTY
1     9     9     2
MADE AND BOTTLED BY
R A V E N S W O O D
SONOMA, CALIFORNIA
CONTAINS SULFITES
ALCOHOL 14.5% BY VOL.

Special events or wine-related programs? Sensory Evaluation, $20, 2:00 P.M. daily by reservation; Create Your Own Zin, $25, 2:00 P.M. daily by reservation; Sunday Barbecue, $20, 11:00 A.M. – 2:00 P.M., June – October.

Wine Club: Zinfomania Wine Club offers monthly shipments. Designation Club offers quarterly shipments. Both offer wine discounts and newsletters.

a Zin lover's knowledge as well as admiration for Ravenswood's hands-on, old-fashioned techniques. "Just the way it was done a hundred years ago," says the guide, adding that if they need modern technology they are glad it is available.

Moving to the fermentation room, you'll see the open-top redwood fermenters that look like hot tubs. Here the red wines spend ten to twelve days fermenting in their own wild yeasts. Three to four times a day, the cap of skins that floats to the top is punched down. When fermentation ceases and the skins sink to the bottom, the wine is left a couple of weeks longer with the skins. This process of extended maceration is a typical Bordeaux technique to extract as much of the flavor and color from the skins as possible.

The most fun part of the tour is a trek into the barrel room to sample the recent vintages by vineyard. For some visitors this experience is like receiving a sacrament. As the guide climbs to a selected barrel, he dips in the "wine thief" he's been carrying, extracts a tubeful, and

releases some into the glass you've been toting through the tour.

This preview of vintages yet to be released titillates the Zinfandel devotees on the tour. While Zinfandel may be what brought you here, other varietals such as Chardonnay, Merlot, and Cabernet Sauvignon are available for tasting, as are Bordeaux varietals, vineyard designates, and well-priced Vintner's Blends.

At the tasting bar, the conversation builds to a glass-raising bravado. It's appropriate when a self-congratulatory toast of allegiance is made to the gutsy approach that has indeed kept wimpiness out of Ravenswood wines.

# St. Francis Winery & Vineyards

St. Francis Winery & Vineyards
100 Pythian Road
Santa Rosa, CA 95409
800-543-7713; 707-833-4666
Fax: 707-833-1394
Website: stfranciswine.com
Email: info@stfranciswine.com

Winemaker: Tom Mackey
Winery owner: Kopf family

## Access

Location: From Highway 101 north, take the Highway 12 exit east toward Sonoma. Continue on Highway 12 for 6 miles from Santa Rosa to the Pythian Road stoplight. Turn left; the winery entrance is on the right. From the town of Sonoma, head north on Highway 12 past Kenwood to the Pythian Road stoplight. Turn right into the parking lot.

Hours open for visits and tastings: 11:00 A.M. – 5:00 P.M. daily, except major holidays.

## Tastings and Tours

Charge for tasting? Yes. $5 for 4 wines; $20 for Patron's Reserve Wine & Food Tasting.

Appointment necessary for tour? Yes; see below.

Tours: For groups of 10 by appointment.

Typical wines offered: Chardonnay, Viognier; Cabernet Franc, Cabernet Sauvignon, Merlot, Petite Sirah, Syrah, Zinfandel; Meritage blend; Port.

Sales of wine-related items? Yes, including logo clothing, Sonoma-made condiments, and more.

## Picnics and Programs

Picnic area open to the public? No.

Picnic ingredients sold in Tasting Room? No.

Special events or wine-related programs? Monthly winemaker dinners; guest chef series winery dinners; cooking demonstrations & lunch; Holiday Open House in November; Heart of Sonoma ☞

With its mission architecture and classic bell tower, St. Francis Winery sits amid the vines at Wild Oak Vineyard in Sonoma Valley like it's always been there. Built in 2001, the relatively new visitor's center of this over thirty-year-old winery conveys a sense of respect for the early California missions established by the friars of its namesake. Utilizing the mission style's warm tones, combination of wood and glass, and simplicity of design, St. Francis Winery combines the best of the historic with a contemporary flair for space and showcasing the vineyard setting. And its food and wine program is one of the best in the wine country.

A favorite time to visit is late afternoon, when the honey-colored winery glows in the setting sun. As you walk across the bridge over crushed granite and bricks between lavender and roses, stop and look up at the bell tower. A plaque on the wall gives the bell's pedigree. It was cast by the oldest foundry in Italy and was blessed in the Piazza della Basilica of St. Francis of Assisi. It rings regularly throughout the day.

Founders Joe Martin and Lloyd Canton planted grapes in 1971 at the Behler Ranch just down the road. When they started making wine in 1979, they named the winery after the Franciscan friars who planted wine grapes at their missions in California. Winemaker Tom Mackey has been here since 1983. In demand as a speaker and wine judge, in 2001 he was honored as Winemaker of the Year by the International Wine Challenge. Known in some circles as a master of Merlot, he is also responsible for the award-winning full-flavored Cabernet, Zinfandel, Meritage blend, Syrah, and Port. Best known these days for "big reds," St. Francis also produces a food-friendly Chardonnay.

As you enter the grand tasting room with its 25-foot-high ceilings, you'll probably smell something cooking. The visitor's center offers one of the best culinary explorations that can be found on a daily basis in the wine country. As one of the wineries in the growing trend to have a resident chef, St. Francis is committed to its wine and food program. Chef Todd Muir initiated the program to show how St. Francis's "big reds" go with food.

You can begin your tasting at the long wood bar in the main room. In winter a fire blazing in the fireplace adds a coziness to the grand space. A small fee, applied to any wine purchase, introduces you to the breadth and depth of St. Francis wines. In support of responsible hospitality, complimentary beverages are provided for your designated driver. Stroll around the room and catch the view from the windows of the great lawn and adjacent vineyards. The large buildings closer to the mountains are the winery.

I recommend purchasing the Patron's Reserve guided wine and appetizer tasting and moving into the VIP Reserve Room. The menu changes seasonally, and it's worth it to see how much flavor the chef puts into each morsel to taste with the selected wines. A fall sampling might be slices of Asian Shrimp Sausage with the Behler Chardonnay, Wild Mushroom and Roasted Garlic Tart with Behler Ranch Merlot, and Point Reyes Blue Cheese and Fig Preserve on top of crostini with Lagomarsino Vineyard Cabernet Franc. When the chef is on hand, engage him in a conversation on his pairings. His task of meeting the big flavors of St. Francis wines is easily accomplished as he explains how a bit of acid or sweetness here and there help tame the tannins, rendering the wine velvety-smooth in harmonious complement. Standing at the beautiful bar in the library-like room, you can sip, taste, and converse while watching the last of the sun's glow against the mountain backdrop.

Barrel Tasting in March; Sonoma Valley Festival of the Lights in December; wedding and event space.

Wine Club: Patrons Wine Club offers 8 wine shipments per year. Zinfantastic Wine Club offers 6 shipments. Both offer discounts on wine and merchandise, complimentary tastings, and discounts on events.

# Sebastiani Vineyards & Winery

Sebastiani Vineyards & Winery
389 Fourth Street
P.O. Box AA
Sonoma, CA 95476
707-933-3230
Fax: 707-933-3390
Website: sebastiani.com
Email: info@sebastiani.com

Winemaker: Mark Lyon
Winery owners: The Cuneo and
Sebastiani families

**Access**
Location: In the town of Sonoma.
From East Spain Street on the north
side of the Plaza, proceed 3 blocks
east and turn left on Fourth Street.
The tasting room and parking lot are
on the right.

Hours open for visits and tastings:
10:00 A.M. – 5:00 P.M. daily,
except major holidays.

**Tastings and Tours**
Charge for tasting? Complimentary
for selected wines; $6 – $15 for
flights, which include 3 wines and a
souvenir logo glass.

Appointment necessary for tour?
No.

Tours: Complimentary self-guided.
Guided historical tours, $5,
Monday – Friday 11:00 A.M.,
1:00 P.M. & 3:00 P.M.; trolley
tours, $7.50, Thursday – Sunday
2:00 P.M. (weather permitting); ☞

Established in 1904, Sebastiani is only two blocks away from the northernmost California mission, San Francisco Solano de Sonoma. The mission vineyards, first planted in 1825, were purchased by founder Samuele Sebastiani in the early 1900s. The wine from *Criolla*, the mission grape, never had a great following, but Sebastiani keeps one old vine growing in the old vineyard.

With respect for preserving the family history as well as the legacy of early Sonoma viticulture, the hundred-year-old winery recently moved into the twenty-first century on several levels. Sebastiani, led by the founder's granddaughter, downsized from a six-million-case operation to around 180,000 cases, with a new commitment to high-quality, handcrafted wines. A beautiful, spacious room now houses the treasured carved wine barrels and other historical artifacts. Sebastiani also offers a multitude of educational tours and tasting programs.

In good weather, one way to begin experiencing Sebastiani's history is to take the trolley tour. The tour brings you through the downtown plaza past the old barracks and City Hall, then to General Vallejo's home before circling back to the renowned Cherry Block Vineyard, whose name comes from the combination of cherry trees and vines planted here by Samuele in 1919. Replanted in 1961, the twenty-eight acres, mostly Cabernet with some Merlot, yield the perfect environment for Sebastiani's flagship wine.

Stepping into the tasting room, you'll find yourself in a fabulous gift shop stocked with beautiful items, from books and linens to wine racks and tableware. The sixty-foot bar under the ceiling arches, however, gives away the primary purpose of the room.

I recommend taking the tour before going to the bar. It feels appropriate to learn the history of Sebastiani and see the old barrels, press, and redwood tanks. Knowing that the wine evolved from a hundred years of hard work adds to the sensory experience of that first taste. Tours can be taken with guides or you can take your own stroll among the carved barrels.

Founder Samuele Sebastiani emigrated from Italy in 1895. In 1904, when he started the winery, the bulk of his wine was made for others. It wasn't until his son August (Gus) and Gus's wife Sylvia took over in 1954 that Sebastiani wines became known by their own label. Gus died in 1980 and Sylvia passed away in 2003.

The first stop on the guided tour is the Sonoma Room, framed by the original winery's 17-inch-thick rock walls. The recent multimillion-dollar reconstruction meant reinforcing the old walls while maintaining their picturesque integrity. In this stuccoed room with its vaulted ceiling, a walk-in fireplace at one end is decorated with a pastel mural of old Sonoma on the wall around it. Continuing into the Radius Room, you'll see the barrel that held Sebastiani's first five hundred gallons of Zinfandel and the original press and crusher.

In the barrel room, adjacent to the tasting room, the magnificent carvings are available for viewing any time the winery is open. All of the carvings were done by Earle Brown, a retired signmaker and friend of Gus

specialty tours for groups of 6 or more. No charge for children under 12.

Typical wines offered: Chardonnay, Symphony; Barbera, Cabernet Franc, Cabernet Sauvignon, Merlot, Pinot Noir, Zinfandel; Bordeaux blend; Grappa (not for tasting).

Sales of wine-related items? Yes, including an emporium of Italian dishes, linens, food items, books, and more.

Picnics and Programs
Picnic area open to the public? Yes.

Picnic ingredients sold in Tasting Room? No, but there is a huge variety of Sebastiani-brand condiments, plus vinegars, books, and more. Cheese and bread and other picnic items available at Sebastiani on the Square a few blocks away.

Special events or wine-related programs? Wine Component Tasting Seminar, $20; Soil to Bottle Seminar, $20. Both are offered daily for 4 or more by appointment. For seasonal events such as Mother's Day, Wine & Chocolate, see website for schedule.

Wine Club: Cherry Block Club offers several tiers that include wine shipments, discounts, and special events. See website for details.

Sebastiani. He chiseled the round caps and barrel ends for Sebastiani between 1967 and 1984. One of his final masterpieces was a portrait of himself as Bacchus, but his face is also apparent in some of the other carvings. Most of the motifs are from nature, many of grapes and wild birds. Gus was a patron of wildlife and bird preservation, and must have passed on that gene to his son Sam, whose winery Viansa in Carneros includes a wetlands and a bird preserve. Many of the decorative caps were placed on the sides of five-thousand-gallon upright redwood tanks. There are three hundred carvings around the winery, including twelve on display here that show the vineyard calendar: renditions of activities from pruning and racking to suckering and bottling.

The magnificent barrel with the stairs going around it holds sixty thousand gallons. If you and a string of solely designated descendants had one glass of wine every day, according to the guide, this barrel would last eight hundred years.

A bottle of wine, on the other hand, pours about ten tasting samples. At the tasting room bar, complimentary sips of Sebastiani's Chardonnay and Cabernet are at the ready. There is also a menu of choices ranging from flights featuring Sonoma County–grown varietals to appellation- and vineyard-designates. Each has a different price. Call ahead to find out what other hospitality programs are taking place, or personalize one for yourself and some friends. Besides its history, Sebastiani features a wealth of food and wine events and educational seminars.

If that isn't enough, Sebastiani on the Square in downtown Sonoma offers a tasting bar, wine sales, food, and, on the weekends, music.

# Viansa Winery & Italian Marketplace

**Viansa Winery & Italian Marketplace**
25200 Arnold Drive
Sonoma Valley, CA 95476
800-995-4740; 707-935-4700
Fax: 707-996-4632
Website: viansa.com
Email: tuscan@viansa.com

Winemaker: Sam Sebastiani
Winery owners: Vicki and Sam Sebastiani

### Access
Location: About 6 miles south of Sonoma. From Highway 101 take Highway 37 or 116 to the east (from Highway 80 take 37 to the west). Turn onto Highway 121 and proceed about 4 miles from either direction to the entrance on the east side of the road.

Hours open for visits and tastings: 10:00 A.M. – 5:00 P.M. daily, except major holidays.

### Tastings and Tours
Charge for tasting? Complimentary for 4 wines. $5 for premier wine selection. Wines also available by the glass for a fee.

Appointment necessary for tour? No.

Tours: $5, 11:00 A.M. & 2:00 P.M. daily, includes tasting. Tours of Wetlands February – May, weather permitting.

Typical wines offered: Sparkling wine: Bisol Brut; Arneis, Chardonnay, Muscat Canelli, Pinot Grigio, Sauvignon Blanc, Tocai Friulano, Vernaccia; Rosato (Rosé); Aleatico, Barbera, Cabernet Franc, Cabernet Sauvignon, Dolcetto, Freisa, Merlot, Nebbiolo, Prindelo, Sangiovese, Zinfandel; Grappa.

Sales of wine-related items? Yes, an entire marketplace of food, dishes, books, and other gourmet items.

### Picnics and Programs
Picnic area open to the public? Yes.

Picnic ingredients sold in Tasting Room? Yes, a complete deli

Around a vineyard-lined jog of Highway 121 less than an hour from San Francisco, Viansa Winery & Italian Marketplace appears like an Italian villa perched on a Tuscan hilltop. Herb gardens at the entrance could be on the outskirts of Lucca. A welcoming opera or piece from Vivaldi resonates from speakers in the entry courtyard, which doubles as the crush pad during harvest. This is the place for lovers of freshly made Italian antipasti and hand-crafted Italian-style wines, for birdwatchers, and for anyone who appreciates attention to detail.

Italian right down to the door hinges and the frescoes, Viansa is the creation of Vicki and Sam Sebastiani. The name comes from a combination of Vicki and Sam (*vi*-and-*sa*), whose commitment to wine with food has produced a winery like no other. Vicki is the inspiration behind the daily menu of salads and pastas in the deli case as well as the sauces and preserves in the marketplace. Sam is a third-generation winemaker in Sonoma County. He specializes in blends of Italian varietals such as Barbera, Trebbiano, Vernaccia, Sangiovese, Dolcetto, and Nebbiolo. And Viansa pays tribute to its ancestors, both Italians and the Native Americans who once lived on the property, by saluting them during the seasons and referencing them on its labels. Lorenzo, a blend of Cabernet Franc and Merlot, is named for Sam's great-grandfather and comes in an amphora-shaped bottle. Ossidiana, a premier blend of Cabernet Franc and Cabernet Sauvignon, is Italian for obsidian, and commemorates an arrowhead found on the property.

Tours begin in the courtyard, where you'll be introduced to this special place. "We are not a large production winery," your guide will tell you, adding that they have the smallest crusher in the wine country. That's because small lots of individual varietals are made and kept separate until it's time to blend. In most wineries the crusher is a monolithic piece of machinery, but the one here is small enough to be stored over the fermentation tanks.

If you come during harvest, all the crush equipment and the bins of grapes will be out in the courtyard. Sit in the loggia, an Italian waiting room, for an intimate look at the hands-on processes. Taste the grapes hot from the vines and the juice straight from the press.

To get into the cellar you pass through ten-foot arched doors made from nineteenth-century barrels. The door hinges are the first example of Viansa's attention to detail. Three coppery-green hinges are embellished with different grape leaves. The top one is Cabernet, the middle Chardonnay, and the bottom is Sauvignon Blanc.

The first stop is the fermentation room, which has no equal in the wine country. Ten five-hundred-gallon tanks lie horizontally behind a stuccoed façade. Only the ends of the tanks, looking like stainless-steel kettle lids, are visible. Above the lids are colorful tiles, each with a hand-painted scene related to winemaking.

In the next room Viansa's red wines are being aged in beautifully carved oak casks. Doors on either side lead to dining rooms used for group tours and other entertainment. From here the circular staircase leads to the marketplace, of hot and cold entrées, salads, frittatas, prosciutto, calzone, antipasti, plus cheese, condiments, bread, crackers, and sweets.

Special events or wine-related programs? April in Carneros; Holiday in Carneros in November; group tours have food as well as wine tastings. Catered dinners, picnics, and weddings.

Wine Club: Tuscan Club members receive monthly shipments of wine, food, and recipes, or food and recipes, or wine only, plus special case discounts, reserved dining areas, and private tours. See website for details.

with marble tasting bars at either end providing a sample of the finished product.

The optimum way to taste the robust wines at Viansa is with a little bread and one of Vicki's bold antipasti, some cheese, a sandwich, or a salad outside at the picnic tables. The tables are shaded by rows of olive trees, and the view up the Carneros toward Sonoma Valley is awesome. Below is the county's largest man-made wetlands and nature preserve, a project that took Sam two years to get approved.

Ducks Unlimited oversees the preserve. Its members, as well as birders from the University of California at Davis, have counted over twelve thousand birds and sixty species on the property, including blue herons, mallards,

egrets, Canadian geese, and golden eagles. The water has also attracted turtles and otters.

You won't need a picnic basket to spend the afternoon at Viansa, but carrying along a market basket will add to the feeling of having been on a short, stimulating vacation in the Italian countryside. And you can even finish your visit with a cappuccino!

# Northern
# Sonoma County

# Alexander Valley Vineyards

**Alexander Valley Vineyards**
8644 Highway 128
P.O. Box 175
Healdsburg, CA 95448
800-888-7209; 707-433-7209
Fax: 707-431-2556
Website: avvwine.com
Email: avv@avvwine.com

Winemaker: Kevin Hall
Winery owner: Harry Wetzel family

**Access**

Location: About 7 miles east of Healdsburg. From Highway 101 north- or southbound take the Dry Creek exit east; turn left at Healdsburg Avenue (the second stoplight), then in about 1½ miles, turn right on Alexander Valley Road. Continue (it turns into Highway 128) for about 5 miles. The winery is on the left.

Hours open for visits and tastings: 10:00 A.M. – 5:00 P.M. daily, except major holidays.

**Tastings and Tours**

Charge for tasting? No, except on small-production lots: $2 – $4 per taste.

Appointment necessary for tour? Yes.

Tours: By appointment.

Typical wines offered: Chardonnay, Gewürztraminer, Viognier, Redemption; Cabernet Franc, Cabernet Sauvignon, Merlot, Pinot Noir, Sangiovese, Syrah, Zinfandel, Sin Zin; Cyrus (Bordeaux blend).

Sales of wine-related items? Yes, including shirts and logo glasses.

**Picnics and Programs**

Picnic area open to the public? Yes.

Picnic ingredients sold in Tasting Room? No.

Special events or wine-related programs? Russian River Wine Road Winter Wineland in January; Russian River Wine Road Barrel Tasting weekend in March; Alexander Valley Taste of the ☞

The homestead of Alexander Valley's namesake is preserved and integrated in one of Sonoma's most secure family wineries. Settled on the expanse between the Mayacamas Mountains and the Russian River, the estate has belonged to only two families since 1847. That's when Cyrus "Aleck" Alexander and his wife Rufena Lucerne received title. In 1962, the property was sold by Alexander's heirs to the Harry and Maggie Wetzel family.

The comfy tasting room with couches and fireplace is on the south end of the stone-and-redwood winery, which means taking a right turn from the driveway. Picnic tables on the deck provide a cool spot to stop at in the swelter of summer. Heat, however, is not a major complaint of the wine-growing locals in Alexander Valley, since it substantially endows the Merlot and Cabernet Sauvignon grapes with the region's acclaimed qualities.

Of the 160 acres planted on the 650-acre estate, over half are devoted to Merlot and Cabernet. Since the land is where the story of this whole valley begins, on the tour your guide starts out with a description of the countryside when Cyrus Alexander scouted it for a wealthy landowner, Captain Fitch, from southern California.

For thousands of years, the peaceful Pomos lived along the valley floor, making their renowned baskets from tules and willows next to the Russian River, hunting game and gathering acorns from the abundant oak trees to

Valley in June; Sin Zin Release Party in October; Food & Wine Affair in November; monthly events throughout the year. Call for schedule or check the website.

Wine Club: Alexander Valley Wine Club members receive shipments 14 times a year, discounts on wine and merchandise, special bottlings, and invitations to special events.

pound into edible meal. The influx of European settlers came on the heels of California's Gold Rush and statehood in the 1850s. By that time Cyrus Alexander had established a ranch for Captain Fitch, who secured a 48,000-acre land grant known as the Sotoyome Grant in 1841.

Upon completion of his contract with Captain Fitch, Cyrus was awarded the 9,000 acres that he chose on the eastern side of the valley. He built the perfect country Victorian you see from the highway and planted wheat, apples, peaches, and grapevines. He also built a church and schoolhouse. He died in 1872 and Rufena died in 1908. Their graves are on the knoll above the winery. You are welcome to take the short hike up to see the gravestones. But the main attraction from the cemetery is the view from this side of Alexander Valley.

The property slowly fell into disrepair after the Alexanders' deaths, and the old Victorian was boarded up when the Wetzels purchased it. The only grapes in the valley at the time were Napa Gamay, Carignane, and a little Zinfandel. In 1966, Harry Wetzel hired Dale Goode as vineyard manager. He was the first in the region to plant Chardonnay, Chenin Blanc, Riesling, and Gewürztraminer, as well as Pinot Noir and Cabernet Sauvignon. He also inaugurated the use of trellises for vine management on the North Coast. Previously all vineyards were head pruned.

By 1973, 125 acres were in full production. Two years later Hank Wetzel, just out of college, produced the first estate wines. When his sister Katie Wetzel Murphy finished at the University of California at Davis, she joined the family business as the director of sales and marketing.

Bucking the trend to ferment Chardonnay in barrels, at Alexander Valley 70 percent ferments in stainless-steel tanks. The Chardonnay remains in the tanks for two to three months without stirring to give it a slightly yeasty component. Then the Chardonnay is blended with the 30 percent that was fermented in oak and aged for six months in French oak barrels. The Pinot Noir ferments in stainless steel and ages in French oak for eight months. Cabernet, Merlot, and the famous Sin Zin with the provocative label are aged in American air-dried oak barrels.

At the end of your tour, or by request if the staff isn't busy, you'll be ushered in to the cave under the hill.

The arched passageways, stacks of barrels, and the heady, rich wine aroma complete the scene. These are working caves where every day wine is being racked and barrels moved around.

Back in the tasting room, throughout spring and summer the Giants' baseball games can be heard on the radio on the mantel. Katie is such a baseball fan that she includes tickets to home-team games as part of her national sales incentives to the winery's distributors, and is meeting her goal of attending games in every American stadium.

Above the fireplace is a painting of the view from the Victorian's porch by Sally Wetzel, Hank and Katie's sister. The legacy that began with the Alexanders 150 years ago continues with the Wetzels' Alexander Valley Vineyards today.

# Chateau Souverain

**Chateau Souverain**

400 Souverain Road, Independence
Lane at Highway 101
P.O. Box 528
Geyserville, CA 95441
888-80-WINES; 707-433-8281
Fax: 707-433-5174
Website: chateausouverain.com

Winemaker: Ed Killian
Winery owner: Beringer Blass Wine
Estates

**Access**

Location: About 7 miles north of
Healdsburg. From Highway 101 take
the Independence Lane exit; the winery is on the west side of the highway.

Hours open for visits and tastings:
10:00 A.M. – 5:00 P.M. daily, except
Christmas and New Year's Day.

**Tastings and Tours**

Charge for tasting? Yes. $3 for 4
wines applied to purchase; special
reserve wines, $2 each.

Appointment necessary for tour? Yes.

Tours: By appointment, $10.

Typical wines offered: Chardonnay,
Sauvignon Blanc, Viognier; Rosé;
Cabernet Sauvignon, Merlot,
Mourvèdre; Pinot Noir, Syrah,
Zinfandel.

Sales of wine-related items? Yes,
including unique selection of shirts,
glasses, books, dishes, linens, and art.

**Picnics and Programs**

Picnic area open to the public? No.

Alexander Valley Grille restaurant on
premises. Lunch daily: 11:30 A.M –
2:30 P.M.; alfresco (lighter fare):
2:30 P.M. – 5:00 P.M.; dinner:
Friday, Saturday & Sunday 5:30
P.M. – 8:00 P.M. Restaurant closed
in January.

Picnic ingredients sold in the tasting
room? Yes, including Sonoma County
artisan cheeses such as Bellwether
Farms Carmody, Spring Hill Jersey
Old World Portuguese, Andante Dairy
Picolo, Point Reyes Blue, Vella Jack;
Souverain Portabella Tapenade, ☞

When the sun rises over the Mayacamas Mountains between Napa and Sonoma Counties, it casts a broad light across the Alexander Valley and shines on Chateau Souverain. You can't miss the palatial landmark reigning sovereignly (as its name implies) from the west side of Alexander Valley. The striking architecture is a blend of French elegance and Sonoma's distinctive hop kiln charm.

As you head up the sweeping driveway lined with honey locust trees, imagine yourself on the way to a French country *auberge* for a little lunch or supper in the vineyards. The image is stunningly close to the truth. Chateau Souverain, with its beautifully appointed restaurant, is like the *auberges* of rural France, where excellent food and a glorious setting create a destination.

Souverain's story begins in Napa County with an emigrant from Switzerland, Fulgenzio Rossini. In 1884, under the Homestead Act, he claimed 160 acres on Howell Mountain, north of St. Helena, where he planted vines and established a winery. In 1943 he sold them to J. Leland Stewart, whose winemaking mentor was the renowned André Tchelistcheff. Stewart named the winery Souverain and won medals for his wines at the state fair.

From 1970 until 1986 Souverain had a string of owners and locations. The original property is now Burgess Cellars, and subsequent property was sold to Rutherford Hill Winery. The Sonoma acreage, acquired in 1973, was the one to retain the Souverain name. The winery built here was designed by architect John Marsh Davis and won an AIA Design Excellence award in 1974.

Souverain's philosophy is to produce the varietals that exemplify the best from each of the county's viticultural appellations. *Terroir*, a French word for earth, is used by wine people to describe the affinity between grape, soil, climate, and exposure that makes certain regions better for certain grape varietals. With its staggering range of geographic and climatic variations, Sonoma County can grow just about any type of grape.

Souverain's label may designate a viticultural appellation such as Dry Creek or Russian River, or a vineyard, such as Sangiacomo. Or a label may say Sonoma County, which means the grapes came from vineyards from several regions in the county.

Here in the hot northern part of Alexander Valley, red grapes, especially Cabernet Sauvignon and the old Italian varieties, do well. The soil is loamy and gravelly and the grapes develop a black cherry flavor. The label on Souverain's Cabernet Sauvignon credits Alexander Valley. The grapes come from Souverain's estate and from neighboring Alexander Valley vineyards.

Although Chardonnay does well in some parts of Alexander Valley, it becomes famous when its home is Russian River, Carneros, or certain areas of Sonoma Valley. Souverain makes an exemplary Russian River Chardonnay. The winery also releases small quantities of Chardonnay with the name of the vineyard in which each was grown.

Dry Creek Valley is known for Zinfandel, and Souverain's is one of the standard-bearers. Russian River and Carneros grow laudable Pinot Noir and Chardonnay grapes, and pockets in the Alexander and Dry Creek

Tomato Tapenade, and Mission Olives; Jimtown Store Fig and Olive Spread, Spicy Olives, and Roasted Vegetables; crackers, nuts, mustards, and Peter Rabbit Chocolates.

Special events or wine-related programs? Crab and Citrus Fest in February; Artisan Cheese and Wine Fest in April; Fall Wild Mushroom and Truffle Fest; Hollyberry Crafts Faire in December. Winery is available for weddings and corporate events.

Wine Club: Vine & Dine Club offers quarterly shipments, discounts on wine and merchandise, VIP dinner and vineyard tour; complimentary glass of wine and olives in café; invitations to special dinners and "Shadow the Chef" cooking classes; plus recipes and discounts to Souverain's food and wine festivals. See website for details.

Valleys tout Sauvignon Blanc as their specialty. Seeing those appellations on a label won't guarantee, but does indicate, excellence in the components.

In the tasting room you can sample the subtle differences. As you educate your palate, the nuances that the professionals identify as characteristics of each region become more noticeable. Remember, you don't have to swallow every taste. Don't feel self-conscious about learning to spit. That's how the professionals do it.

Souverain's tasting room is a colorful contrast to the sedate exterior of the winery. A mural in shades of purple and aqua, painted by artist Tony Sheets, wraps around all four walls and depicts a year in the life of a vineyard, with eye-catching highlights in gold and bronze.

Recognizing that the best way to taste wine is with food, Chateau Souverain opened its own restaurant, serving lunch daily and dinner on the weekends. While the prices are reasonable, the setting is purely upmarket, as is the quality of the food by Chef Martin Courtman. You can sink into upholstered chairs at linen-covered tables next to the blazing fireplace in the winter, or eat alfresco on the terrace in summer. Either way, the panorama across Alexander Valley is exquisite. If you dine at day's end, you'll see the last of the sun's rays catching the top of the chateau's roof turrets before night's shadow envelops them. Almost like an *auberge* in France.

# Dry Creek Vineyard

**Dry Creek Vineyard**
3770 Lambert Bridge Road
Healdsburg, CA 95448
800-864-9463; 707-433-1000
Fax: 707-433-5329
Website: drycreekvineyard.com
Email: dcv@drycreekvineyard.com

Winemaker: Bill Knuttel
Winery owners: David Stare,
founder; Don and Kim Stare Wallace

**Access**
Location: About 4½ miles west of
Healdsburg. From Highway 101
take the Dry Creek Road exit; follow
it to the west 3½ miles, and turn
right on Lambert Bridge Road. The
winery is on the left.

Hours open for visits and tastings:
10:30 A.M – 4:30 P.M. daily,
except New Year's Eve and Day,
Easter, July 4th, Thanksgiving, and
Christmas Eve and Day.

**Tastings and Tours**
Charge for tasting? Not for regular
list. Reserve tasting in cellar, $5,
includes logo wineglass.

Appointment necessary for tour?
No tour.

Typical wines offered: Chardonnay,
Fumé Blanc, Dry Chenin Blanc;
Cabernet Sauvignon, Meritage,
Zinfandel; Late Harvest Sauvignon
Blanc and Zinfandel.

A favorite tasting room for visitors and locals alike, Dry Creek Vineyard deserves the allegiance of its fans. One reason for this is the professionalism and knowledge of the staff. Another is the consistent quality of the wines. This family-owned winery exudes a relaxed atmosphere and a sophistication that is underscored by its leadership in the industry. Credit goes to founder David Stare, his daughter Kim, and his son-in-law Don Wallace, who are raising their children to become part of the winery.

At the time Dry Creek Vineyard was founded in 1972, only three other wineries, mostly producers of bulk wines, were in the valley. It was the first new winery in Dry Creek since the end of Prohibition. Today there are forty-five wineries. David was instrumental in getting Dry Creek the status of an appellation and the first to put "Dry Creek Valley" on his label. Dry Creek was also the first winery to have a sailboat as a logo on its label. Hang on a minute for that part of the story.

A graduate of MIT and Northwestern University, David is an accomplished industrial engineer. When he moved from Baltimore to California in 1971, he brought with him an infatuation with Pouilly Fumé and Sancerre, the white wines of the Loire Valley. He also brought a vow to learn how to make them, enrolling in oenology and viticulture courses at the University of California at Davis. A year later he produced his first vintage, thirteen hundred cases of Fumé Blanc, Chardonnay, and Dry Chenin Blanc. By 1973 he had bonded his winery in the heart of the Dry Creek Valley.

Of the winery's six varietals, Zinfandel and Cabernet Sauvignon reign, but Fumé Blanc has a particularly loyal following. Dry Creek Vineyard was the first Sonoma County winery to concentrate on Sauvignon Blanc as a varietal. Here it is labeled Fumé Blanc, the name first used by Robert Mondavi to designate a dry Sauvignon Blanc. While Sauvignon Blanc is often described by critics as tasting "grassy," and some vintners try to minimize that characteristic, "grassiness" is not a negative word here. In fact, that very quality, coupled with the complex depth that the grape develops, is what aroused David's love of the wines in the Loire. He describes the flavor of his wine as "straightforward sass with a crisp finish." Given its French inspiration, the name is most appropriate at Dry Creek Vineyards, which today is one of the leading producers of Sauvignon Blanc in the United States.

You will always learn something from the staff at this busy winery, which produces a hundred thousand cases a year. They'll tell you it takes four clusters of grapes to make one bottle of wine. A one-acre vineyard here yields four to six tons of grapes; one ton equals 180 gallons, which equals three barrels, or sixty-five cases.

Why the sailboat? David's passion is sailing. He doesn't have a sailboat any more, but Dry Creek Vineyards is a frequent supporter of sailing events, maritime campaigns, and foundations around the country. From the irony of a boat on a "dry creek" (which the nearby northern tributary of the Russian River isn't) comes the winery's customer recognition. Throughout the years, Dry Creek has commissioned dozens of watercolor paintings with the sailboat theme as labels for its reserve wines.

Dry Creek Vineyard is open for visitors year-round. The cozy tasting room is always a shopper's paradise of carefully selected merchandise. During winter deluges the tasting room is a warm harbor in the glow of the huge stone fireplace. In the springtime, wildflowers bloom as cover crops between the budding vines. At harvest you have a clear view of the crushing and juicing, which take place between the parking lot and the winery. And when the madness of crush is over, the valley floor surrounding the winery is a multicolored paisley carpet in seasonal transition.

One spring day in the tasting room, a suntanned man with a straw hat came in with an armload of the gigantic orange, yellow, pink, and red tulips he raises and trucks into San Francisco to sell at the flower mart. He brought them in exchange for the pomace he had hauled from the winery after crush. If you aren't familiar with pomace, the staff will explain that it is the stems, seeds, and skins left over from pressing the grapes, and a perfect garden mulch.

In addition to being a fount of information, the winery, with its country French architecture, always-blooming flower garden, and intimate scale, is a favorite picnic site in Sonoma County.

Sales of wine-related items? Yes, including glasses, shirts, books, linens, dishes, and jewelry.

**Picnics and Programs**
Picnic area open to the public? Yes.

Picnic ingredients sold in Tasting Room? No, but Dry Creek Store with complete deli is just up the road.

Special events or wine-related programs? Russian River Wine Road Winter Wineland in January; Russian River Wine Road Barrel Tasting in March; Passport to Dry Creek Valley in April; Holiday Open House in December.

Wine Club: Vintner's Select Club members receive 4 wine shipments annually, invitations to special tastings and dinners, and extra wine discounts. VIP Club receives the same plus 2 more shipments.

# Ferrari-Carano Vineyards & Winery

Ten thousand colorful tulips are a draw here in the spring. Afterward, the rhododendrons bloom. And hundreds of roses flower in summer and fall. Pansies, ranunculus, petunias, and marigolds alternate as colorful borders around Ferrari-Carano's pathways and ponds throughout the year. Named Villa Fiore, which means "house of flowers," the visitor's center, designed by owners Don and Rhonda Carano, commemorates their Italian heritage and love of good wine with food and friends. Their passion is also showcased as the owners of the famed John Ash Restaurant and Vintners Inn in Santa Rosa and the Eldorado Hotel/Casino in Reno.

You might be content to come to Ferrari-Carano to see the five acres of theme gardens, rest in a gazebo, gaze at a waterfall, or meander from one verdant section to another. Equally spectacular, however, is tasting the wine in the villa of the century, a focal point of irresistible appeal in this northern stretch of Dry Creek Valley.

Before you enter the showplace tasting room, pause on the terrace at the entrance. The entire picture—vineyards, foothills, winery, and gardens—adds to the feeling that you have just arrived at a villa outside of Florence. Under the terrace, one of the most beautiful barrel cellars in the world is kept cool by the gardens and sloping berm.

**Ferrari-Carano Vineyards & Winery**
8761 Dry Creek Road
P.O. Box 1549
Healdsburg, CA 95448
800-831-0381; 707-433-6700
Fax: 707-431-1742
Website: ferrari-carano.com
Email: customerservice@
fcwinery .com

Winemaker: George Bursick
Winery owners: Don and Rhonda
Carano

**Access**
Location: About 9 miles northwest of Healdsburg. From Highway 101 take the Dry Creek Road exit, turn west, and continue for 9 miles. The winery is on the left.

Hours open for visits and tastings: 10:00 A.M. – 5:00 P.M. daily, except major holidays.

**Tastings and Tours**
Charge for tasting? Yes. $3 applied to purchase; list of reserve wines for $15.

Appointment necessary for tour? Yes, with a guide; self-guided tours of cellar and gardens any time.

Tours: 10:00 A.M. Monday – Friday by reservation only.

Typical wines offered: Chardonnay, Fumé Blanc; Cabernet Sauvignon, Merlot, Syrah, Zinfandel; Tresor (Bordeaux blend), ☛

SIENA (Sangiovese-Cabernet Sauvignon blend); late-harvest signature wines.

Sales of wine-related items? Yes, extensive selection of packaged foods and preserves, clothes including vests and ties, gardening tools and art, dishes, linens, and more.

**Picnics and Programs**
Picnic area open to the public? No.

Picnic ingredients sold in Tasting Room? No.

Special events or wine-related programs? Tasting Experience in the Italian Cellar, $25, by appointment for 6 or more; Passport to Dry Creek in April. Call for schedule of cooking classes with Rhonda, and other educational and culinary events. Tulip Hotline, 707-433-5349, updated weekly in the early spring.

Wine Club: Circle of Friends presents 2 options. Classic offers wine shipments of 1 red and 1 white 3 times a year. Cellar Master offers 2 red wines 3 times a year. Both offer wine discounts, member-only events, travel offers including John Ash & Co. and Vintners Inn.

Inside the tasting room, known as the Wine Shop, the Italian theme is elaborated in a shopper's paradise of wine, food products including estate-grown olive oil, clothes, and even garden tools. The birds-eye maple trim and cabinets, faux-marbled walls, and marbleized and etched floor are on permanent exhibit, created by local artisans specializing in antique reproduction who spent weeks on the project. Look closely at the details and stand back to see the whole effect.

In addition to the sixty acres surrounding the villa and winery, the Caranos own twenty-five hundred vineyard acres on eighteen sites, from Dry Creek and Alexander Valleys to Knight's Valley, which is also in Sonoma County, all the way to Carneros and the Napa County border. Terrain includes hillside, bench land, and valley floor, and a variety of grapes is grown on each, which is why so many different lots are available for the Chardonnay, as well as for the Fumé Blanc, Merlot, Cabernet Sauvignon, and Zinfandel.

A tour with a guide is by appointment and will take you on a complete circuit of the grounds and the winery. On the walk around the buildings you'll see a cork tree and a weeping cherry as you pass the outdoor kitchen on the way to the crush pad.

At the crush pad a must chiller drops the temperature of white grapes to 30°F in two minutes. A horizontal rotary fermenter holds twelve to twenty tons of red grapes and operates by gently rotating the grapes inside the drum to release the juice. The intensely flavored fruit grown on the Caranos' mountain vineyards is rotated twice a day, while the lighter-flavored valley grapes are rotated every thirty minutes to extract as much flavor as desired.

Moving inside to the fermentation room, where brushed stainless-steel tanks gleam, you won't see the dimpled glycol-filled jackets that typically encircle fermentation tanks for temperature control. Here the jackets have been put on the backs of the tanks, where they have been found to be more efficient. As the guide explains, "the hot chases the cold, causing actual movement of the wine inside. We discovered these tanks to be 40 percent more energy-efficient than those with the bands around them."

After the cold of the stainless-tank-filled rooms, entering the barrel room feels as warm as it looks. The cream-colored double-vaulted ceiling glows from lighting recessed in the pillars. From an elevated veranda with a brass railing you look out over eleven hundred French oak barrels, stacked two and three high. The center of each, which holds red wine for up to three years, is carefully painted with a red wine stripe.

A view of the barrel room is also accessible from the opposite end, which you can reach on your own down the stairs from the tasting room. Hand-painted wall frescoes on the lower level and in the ceiling dome in the main lobby of the building depict the Italian winemaking legacy and the Caranos' heritage. From the architecture and gardens to such vineyard names as Dell'Oro, La Strada, and Allegro to the labels on the wines, Ferrari-Carano is unmistakably Italian.

# Field Stone Winery

**Field Stone Winery**
10075 Highway 128
Healdsburg, CA 95448
707-433-7266
Fax: 707-433-2231
Website: fieldstonewinery.com
Email: fieldstone1@earthlink.net

Winemaker: Tom Milligan
Winery owners: Katrina and John Staten

**Access**
Location: About 7 miles east of Healdsburg. From Highway 101 north- or southbound take the Dry Creek Road exit east. Turn left at Healdsburg Avenue (the second stoplight), and in about 1½ miles turn right on Alexander Valley Road. Continue (it turns into Highway 128) for about 6 miles. The winery is on the right.

Hours open for visits and tastings: 10:00 A.M. – 5:00 P.M. daily, except major holidays.

**Tastings and Tours**
Charge for tasting? No.

Appointment necessary for tour? Yes.

Typical wines offered: Chardonnay, Gewürztraminer, Sauvignon Blanc, Viognier; Cabernet Sauvignon, Merlot, Petite Sirah, Sangiovese, and in some years a California-style vintage Port.

Field Stone Winery appeals to romantics who dream of what the classic winery should look like. Located on the west side of Highway 128 between Geyserville and Calistoga, Field Stone's small subterranean cellar, surrounded by a forest of valley oaks, is a vision of the perfect wine cellar.

Everything is within reach in the compact setup. Inside, you walk past the bottling line and between barrels to get to the tiny redwood-paneled tasting room. Above the winery is the crush pad, with its clever gravity-flow system into the fermentation room. A horse named Shawnee, a couple of ducks, and a few chickens add to the inviting scene, as do the gnarly Petite Sirah grapevines planted in 1894, which continue to produce big, dark, beautiful fruit for Field Stone's flagship wine and vintage Port. French clones of Cabernet Sauvignon and Merlot also grow around the winery.

You can make an appointment for an official tour or walk around and immerse yourself in a personal-fantasy tour of the little winery. You'll probably run into the owner, John Staten, or the winemaker, and they'll be quick to point out the hard work that goes into producing wine. Wine is often being racked or readied for bottling. The Italian-made bottling line runs at various times throughout the year. That's because this is not a "vanilla and chocolate" winery, says the tasting room host. "For a small winery (ten thousand cases) we make small lots of special wines," not the expected lots of one or two.

Field Stone's varietals include a dry Gewürztraminer, Sauvignon Blanc, Chardonnay, Viognier, Merlot, Zinfandel, Petite Sirah, two Cabernet Sauvignons, and a luscious Sangiovese. In addition, there are always one or two special blends available only in the tasting room. Bottles etched with "Happy Valentine's Day" or, for the Big Game, one with "Stanford" and another with "Cal Berkeley" make meaningful gifts.

The winery was founded in 1977 by Wally Johnson, Staten's father-in-law. A former mayor of Berkeley, Johnson was raised on a farm in Iowa and came to the Alexander Valley in the late 1950s to raise cattle. Over the years he planted the newer vineyards. One of his accomplishments was the invention of a mechanical upright harvester. He theorized that to get the full fruit concentration of Chardonnay it should be picked like the corn was for dinner back home. His machine picked and crushed, and the juice was immediately piped into an airtight container right in the vineyard.

After Wally Johnson's untimely death at sixty-six in 1979, his daughter Katrina and her husband John took over the winery. A religious educator and ordained Presbyterian minister, John was a novice to winemaking, so he engaged California's legendary wine authority, André Tchelistcheff, as consulting oenologist. The late Tchelistcheff's eleven years of advice have paid off in the excellence of the wine that John has created from the beginning.

Best known for its red wines, Field Stone's Cabernet clone sources are from the who's who of vineyards. The Cabernet budwood came in 1967 from Napa Valley's prestigious Old Niebaum vineyard and Martha's Vineyard. Alexander Valley's riverbottom soil is gravelly, sandy loam, which provides high yields and intense flavor to red varietals. Coupled with the fog-tempered summer weather, the elements have helped the valley become famous for distinctive red wines.

In what is an unusual move with red wine, the Petite Sirah is blended at harvest with a white grape, Viognier. As the winemaker puts it, "this practice, borrowed from the French Côte Rôtie, allows us to overcome the undesirably harsh, grainy tannins that are often associated with this variety."

While tasting at the redwood bar in the lively tasting room, notice the half-moon-shaped window that looks out at ground level. It offers a mole's view of the picnic area that surrounds the winery. Dozens of handmade round plywood tables are set on barrels with seats perched on poles, resembling a grove of mushrooms or a scene from the Mad Hatter's tea party.

If your basket is packed with ripe cheese and crusty bread, the Petite Sirah is just the accompaniment. In the summer cheese, salami, and crackers are usually stocked in the tasting room.

While checking out the wines, be sure to notice the labels. The exquisitely detailed grape clusters are reproduced from photographs taken by John Staten. Field Stone is the only winery to illustrate the label with the grape that's in the wine. This thoughtful gesture only enhances the sentimental allure of this seductive winery.

Sales of wine-related items? Yes, including shirts and logo glasses.

**Picnics and Programs**
Picnic area open to the public? Yes.

Picnic ingredients sold in Tasting Room? In summer and busy times, including cheese, salami, crackers, pastas, and condiments.

Special events or wine-related programs? Russian River Wine Road Winter Wineland in January; Russian River Wine Road Barrel Tasting in March; Taste of the Valley; Wine & Food Affair in November.

Wine Club: Field Stone Wine Club members receive wine shipments 3 times a year and discounts on wines, and are invited to special events.

# Fritz Winery

**Fritz Winery**
24691 Dutcher Creek Road
Cloverdale, CA 95425
707-894-3389
Fax: 707-894-4781
Website: fritzwinery.com
Email: info@fritzwinery.com

Winemaker: Christina Pällman
Winery owner: Arthur Jay Fritz

**Access**
Location: About 8½ miles from
Healdsburg. From Highway 101
northbound take the Dry Creek
Road exit. Proceed west 9 miles and
turn right on Dutcher Creek Road.
The winery is about 11 miles away
on the left. Watch for the sign. From
Highway 101 southbound take the
Dutcher Creek exit and proceed
about 3 miles to the winery on the
right.

Hours open for visits and tastings:
10:30 A.M. – 4:30 P.M daily,
except major holidays.

**Tastings and Tours**
Charge for tasting? No.

Appointment necessary for tour?
Yes. 🖘

Wineries become known for their exceptional wine, fastidious winemaking, brilliant architecture, outstanding setting, or perhaps environmental principles. Fritz Winery attracts attention on all these counts.

As you drive along the far north end of Dry Creek Valley and turn onto the steep driveway, the winery appears, like no other in Sonoma County. Splayed at an angle across the steep oak-studded hillside, the white stucco front looks like a cross between a Greek tabernacle and a *Flash Gordon* space station.

If you come in spring, my favorite season to visit, a cacophony of mating birds fills the sweet air with tweets, chirps, bleats, and warbles. Geese honk from the pond below and a chorus of crickets renders an intermittent din. A profusion of wildflowers colors the turf roof against the white façade. Everything feels deliciously alive and in motion.

As you climb up the terraced entry to the middle and only visible level of the three-tiered structure, it's worth noting that the three arched doorways are there for a reason. They symbolize the three essentials of good grape growing: sun, soil, and rain.

Before going inside, pause on the black-tiled terrace and turn around to feast on the view. Bird feeders are everywhere, and if bird-watching is an interest, be sure to reserve one of the picnic tables. A golden eagle, red-tailed hawk, grape-loving woodpecker, and an abundance of other resident and migratory birds have been spotted here.

Inside the tasting room, a minimalist approach emphasizes simplicity and classiness. The handcrafted bar with its accordion-pleated base is made of black walnut from nearby Cloverdale. A woodstove in the corner warms the subterranean room during the cool months. From spring through summer the arched doors are open to the terrace.

Burrowing into the hillside to build the winery was a "conservation-conscious decision" made by owner and former international businessman Arthur Jay Fritz, who in 1979 was ahead of his time in striving to make an energy-efficient winery. Terracing the winery on three levels allows a gravity flow of the wine from one production phase to the next. Using the earth for insulation is economical for temperature control.

The steep, wide stairs lined with orange and yellow gazanias lead to the crush pad. Here the Chardonnay grapes get the kind of special attention usually reserved for fine sparkling wine. And that is only the beginning when it comes to the handcrafted winemaking that is now under the tutelage of Arthur's son, Clayton Fritz, who took over as president in 2002.

You may learn about "free-run" juice used for white wines. This means the stems are removed, the grape skins broken, and only the juice that runs out naturally is made into Fritz wine. Red grapes, like the Zinfandel Fritz is famous for, are fermented in open-top fermenters and left to "macerate" in their skins.

Hoses and pipes gravity-feed the juice to the middle level inside the winery. The theory is that the wine has less chance of being aerated by this natural flow than if it is pumped. Aeration affects the flavor and color of the grapes.

Typical wines offered: Chardonnay, Sauvignon Blanc; Carignane, Cabernet Sauvignon, Pinot Noir, Zinfandel; late-harvest Zinfandel.

Sales of wine-related items? Yes, including logo glasses, shirts, cookbooks, and gift baskets.

**Picnics and Programs**
Picnic area open to the public? Yes.

Picnic ingredients sold in Tasting Room? No.

Special events or wine-related programs? Russian River Wine Road Winter Wineland in January; Russian River Wine Road Barrel Tasting in March; Passport open house with music and food in April.

Wine Club: Underground Wine Club includes option of Bottle Club or Case Club shipments, plus member-only savings, special wine offerings, and winery events.

On the tour, following the hoses inside the middle level, you get a sense of this remarkable semicircular building built to follow the curve of the hill. From one open doorway, you can look down on the bottling line on the bottom level. Next, you pass the lab and descend the stairs to the cave, where the barrels are stacked for aging of the Zinfandel and Cabernet and fermenting of some of the Chardonnay.

In addition to being environmentally conscious and sticklers for relatively time-consuming methods, Fritz makes award-winning top-of-the-line wines that are amazingly well priced.

# Geyser Peak Winery

**Geyser Peak Winery**
22281 Chianti Road
Geyserville, CA 95441
800-255-9463; 707-857-9400
Fax: 707-857-9402
Website: geyserpeakwinery.com
Email: info@geyserpeakwinery.com

Winemakers: Daryl Groom, executive winemaker, with Mick Schroeter, Chris Munsell, Ondine Chattan
Winery owner: Jim Beam Brands Co.

**Access**

Location: In Geyserville. From Highway 101 north- or southbound take the Canyon Road exit; turn west on Canyon Road and right on Chianti. The winery is on the left.

Hours open for visits and tastings: 10:00 A.M. – 5:00 P.M. daily, except major holidays.

**Tastings and Tours**

Charge for tasting? Not in main tasting room. Flights in the Reserve Room range from single wines at $2 – $3 to flights ranging from $5 – $10.

Appointment necessary for tour? No tours.

Typical wines offered: Chardonnay, Dry Riesling, Sauvignon Blanc; Cabernet Sauvignon, Meritage, Merlot, Port, Zinfandel; also tasting-room-only releases of Cabernet Franc, Malbec, Petite Verdot; and nonalcoholic grape juice.

Sales of wine-related items? Yes, including shirts, books, dishes, condiments and preserves, and picnic baskets.

**Picnics and Programs**

Picnic area open to the public? Yes.

Picnic ingredients sold in Tasting Room? Yes, including Sonoma Jack cheese, salami, pâté, Jimtown Olive Spread, olives, and crackers.

Special events or wine-related programs? Guided Reserve tasting flights in the upstairs ☞

Winemaking at Geyser Peak has gone on for more than 120 years. The ivy-covered exterior of the stone winery lends an Old World security, as though the winery has been here forever. The consistently high rating of their elegant wines is an accolade that often takes generations to attain. But Geyser Peak, despite a lackluster history of bulk wine and brandy, has risen to the top in a relatively short time.

Named for Geyser Peak, which you can see shooting bursts of steam across the valley from the flagstone courtyard entrance, the winery sits on the west side of northern Alexander Valley. It was founded in 1880 by Augustus Quitzow, who constructed a twenty-thousand-gallon facility in 1892, and sold it seven years later to Edward Walden and Company, a brandy company. A string of ventures, including brandy and vinegar production, sustained it until 1982, when the Henry Trione family from Santa Rosa came along.

When the Triones bought the winery they realized the potential of the hundreds of acres of prime vineyards and decided to concentrate on making premium wines. By 1989 Geyser Peak, affectionately known as "the Peak," was one of the top twenty-five wineries in California. Sold in 1998 to Jim Beam Brands, Geyser Peak continues to rank among the top American wineries, with Australian-born vice president Daryl Groom and winemaker Mick Schroeter at the helm.

The recently remodeled tasting room is a spacious showplace for wine displays, books, and foodstuffs. While you will have a personalized experience at the main tasting bar, in order to immerse yourself in an intimate guided tasting, I recommend heading upstairs to the Reserve Room. Settle into the comfortable upholstered armchairs at round tables for four. Read over the selection of flights, a sampling of three or four wines priced accordingly, which range from all white to Shiraz (a house specialty), from Meritage (another forte) to reserves.

Soft lighting, library-like cherry paneling, mood music, and the picture-window view of the dimly lit barrel room, framed by heavy curtains, create an inviting place to settle in for a serious wine discussion. Each wine is served in a coordinated vessel. For the Shiraz flight, which

features the Australian-named Syrah grape as sparkling, reserve, and Port, you'll begin with a tulip-shaped Riedel flute and end with a "Port pipe." This looks like a mini clear-glass amphora with a strawlike glass sipper. You'll learn how to hold the Australian-made Port glass in your hand to warm it up and then sip it through the pipe.

For the Meritage flight, you get an opportunity to taste three of the lesser known varietals that are added to Cabernet Sauvignon and Merlot, the backbone of Meritage, California's designated Bordeaux-style blends. First you'll sample Malbec, Cabernet Franc, and Petit Verdot and learn about the qualities that each of these wines contributes to the esteemed Reserve Alexandre, Geyser Peak's Meritage blend.

In the main tasting room, you'll have to stand at the bar, but you can still taste most of the wines made here. From the easy-drinking Sauvignon Blanc to the flagship Shiraz, you can go on to compare different Sonoma vineyard selections of Chardonnay and taste world-class Alexander Valley Cabernet Sauvignon.

Along with wine tasting, Geyser Peak is a favorite picnic destination, and the tasting room has cheese, salami, pâté, and crackers always stocked. You are encouraged to bring the whole family, sit on the arbor-covered terrace, and enjoy the expansive view. Vineyards fill the valley, their colors and textures changing with the seasons, alongside the mighty Russian River. And it's always a thrill to watch the steamy geysers spout from the peaks on the horizon.

reserve room; Russian River Wine Road Winter Wineland in January; Russian River Wine Road Barrel Tasting in March; Taste of the Valley in June; Wine & Food Affair in November.

Wine Club: Cellar Door Club offers wine shipments every 6 weeks, special discounts, notice of new and limited releases, invitations to semiannual luncheons, and participation in the annual crush.

# Preston of Dry Creek Winery & Vineyards

**Preston of Dry Creek Winery & Vineyards**
9282 West Dry Creek Road
Healdsburg, CA 95448
800-305-9707; 707-433-3372
Website: prestonvineyards.com
Email: mail@prestonvineyards.com

Winemaker: Matt Norelli
Winery owners: Lou and Susan Preston

**Access**
Location: From north- or south-bound Highway 101, take the Dry Creek exit to the west. Head north on Dry Creek Road for about 8 miles, then turn right at the Preston sign and follow the driveway to the winery.

Hours open for visits and tastings: 11:00 A.M. – 4:30 P.M. daily, except major holidays.

**Tastings and Tours**
Charge for tasting? Yes. $3, applied to purchase.

Appointment necessary for tour? No tours.

Typical wines offered: Sauvignon Blanc, Viognier; Rosé; Barbera, Sangiovese, Syrah, Old Vine Zinfandel; Guadagni Red Zinfandel jug wine (on Sundays only).

Sales of wine-related items? Yes, including estate olives and olive oil, books, and more.

**Picnics and Programs**
Picnic area open to the public? Yes, with purchase of wine.

Picnic ingredients sold in Tasting Room? Yes, including hearth oven bread, olives, cheese, olive oil, and condiments and spreads.

Special events or wine-related programs? Russian River Wine Road Winter Wineland in January; Russian River Wine Road Barrel Tasting in March; and winery-sponsored events. Call the winery or check the website.

Wine Club: i Prestoni Wine Club offers quarterly wine shipments, special discounts, and member-only events.

Something Italian is going on at this winery. It could be the bocce courts, the homemade olive oils, or the *forno*-baked hearth bread. It could be the Barbera wine, the heritage of one of the owners and the winemaker, or the flavors of a lifestyle, one that encourages you to slow down a bit. That's what owners Lou and Susan Preston decided to do after nearly thirty years of building their winery to thirty thousand cases. When they realized that marketing had taken over what they set out to do on their beautiful property in the middle of Dry Creek Valley, they downsized, and now their maximum is eight thousand cases.

"We resized the winery to make it more manageable as a family business," says Lou, the master bread baker, olive curer, and pizza maestro. As one of the founders and first president of the Winegrowers of Dry Creek Valley, he was known to carry the word about this once lesser known grape-growing region on his travels all over the United States. Preston's reputation was built on Rhône varietals and bottlings of small lots of a variety of wines.

Now the Prestons are concentrating on the core varietals of Sauvignon Blanc, Syrah, Zinfandel, and Barbera and their signature blend of Syrah, Mourvèdre, Cinsault, and old vine Carignane. They are in the process of getting organic certification from California Certified Organic Farmers (CCOF). They have planted hedgerows for beneficial insects to live in and, instead of spraying for

weeds, grow cover crops of legumes and clover between the vines. The tractors are fueled by biodiesel and their car runs on vegetable oil. Susan has time for her art, some of which you see hanging in the tasting room.

As you go down the meandering driveway next to the oxbow in the creek, taking it slow is the only way to arrive. Olive trees and grapes have replaced the prunes and pears that once grew on this valley floor property, purchased by the Prestons in the early '70s. The old Zinfandel is still here, and so are the wit and wisdom passed on by the old-time Italian-born neighbors who shepherded, advised, and occasionally approved of the newcomers' ways of planting vines and making wine.

As the vineyards slowly become organically certified, the Prestons welcome visitors to the winery to taste their wines, which still include a proprietary selection of varietals found only at the winery. Lou's crusty bread is usually on hand, and Preston's estate olive oil stands ready to accompany your wine tasting. If you've brought a picnic, you can buy some wine and head out to the tables next to the bocce courts, where one of the old Italian locals might be on hand to give you some pointers, talk about the local wild mushrooms, or simply lend some atmosphere to remind you to take stock of what's important.

To add to the ambience, the wood-fired oven may be going. There are two now; the original one is outside on the way to the bocce courts, and the new one is the centerpiece of a commercial kitchen adjacent to the tasting room. Here Lou and Susan dish up thin-crusted pizza topped with tomatoes and wild mushrooms at events for the Russian River Wine Road or Dry Creek Valley Association.

If you come on a Sunday, you can pick up a three-liter jug of Guadagni Red, a Zinfandel made in honor of one of Preston's neighbors. You can also pick up a flyer about its namesake, Jim Guadagni, then sit back and read about one of those old Italian Americans whose heritage and influence live on at Preston.

# Quivira Estate Vineyards & Winery

**Quivira Estate Vineyards & Winery**
4900 West Dry Creek Road
Healdsburg, CA 95448
800-292-8339; 707-431-8333
Fax: 707-431-1664
Website: quivirawine.com
Email: quivira@quivirawine.com

Winemaker: Grady Wann
Owners: Henry and Holly Wendt

**Access**

Location: From Highway 101 north-
or southbound, take the Dry Creek
Road exit to the west. Follow it for
3½ miles and turn left on Lambert
Bridge Road, then right on West Dry
Creek Road. The winery is half a
mile on the right.

Hours open for visits and tastings:
11:00 A.M. – 5:00 P.M. daily,
except major holidays.

**Tastings and Tours**

Charge for tasting? No.

Appointment necessary for tour?
Reservations required.

Typical wines offered: Sauvignon
Blanc, Grenache, Mourvèdre Rosé,
Petite Sirah, Syrah, Zinfandel (sev-
eral vineyard designates).

Sales of wine-related items? Yes,
including books, logo clothing,
and more.

**Picnics and Programs**

Picnic area open to the public? Yes,
on the redwood and olive tree –
shaded patio next to the vineyard.

Picnic ingredients sold in Tasting
Room? No.

Special events or wine-related
programs? Russian River Wine Road
Winter Wineland in January;
Fondue Fridays in February;
Russian River Wine Road Barrel
Tasting in March; many others.
Check the website or call the tasting
room.

Wine Club: Club Q offers wine shipments 3 times a year, discounts on
all purchases, barrel tastings,
recipes, new release parties, and
discounts on special winery events.

Quivira stands out as one of the memorable stops in Dry Creek Valley, where narrow country lanes are flanked by vineyards, olive trees, and family-owned wineries. Reminiscent of the Provençal countryside, Dry Creek Valley is a place to linger, which makes touring conducive to a round trip by bicycle as well as by slow-moving car. Take Dry Creek Road one way and West Dry Creek Road the other.

Quivira, on West Dry Creek Road, is a perfect place to tour during crush. Everything happens within sight behind the tasting room, where a chalkboard announces the daily schedule, such as "Harvest has begun with the Sauvignon Blanc." At the crush pad, grapes are unloaded into the crusher, juice flows out into fermenters, and the air is thick with the sweet, ripe aroma.

On the guided tour or on your own, you can walk along Wine Creek, a tributary to Dry Creek, which flows into the Russian River. The creek is being meticulously restored in partnership with Trout Unlimited. After years of mining scoured many of the local creek beds such as this, it's rewarding to enjoy the riparian regrowth. One sight on the tour is the landmark historic barn on West Dry Creek Road. It is located next to Fig Tree Vineyard, where the Sauvignon Blanc and some Semillon grow to be made into Quivira's excellent blend. The ninety acres of vines are predominantly planted to Zinfandel and Sauvignon Blanc, Quivira's specialties.

Since the winery's name is intriguing, you should know that Quivira's owners, Henry and Holly Wendt, are history buffs. The name came from the story of the Spanish explorer Cabrillo, who was sure he would find other kingdoms as rich and cultured as that of the Aztecs. Following the tale of an Indian who told him of a wealthy gilded place far north, Cabrillo went in search of a magi-

cal place called "Quivira," which between 1569 and 1752 was situated on maps to the north of San Francisco, near a large river. The Wendts collect old maps, and had one showing Quivira. In 1981, when the Wendts purchased property in Dry Creek Valley, they found this historical myth compelling enough to name their winery Quivira.

Back in the tasting room, friendly staff are on hand to guide you. From the beautiful handcrafted curved bar, raise your glass to the view through the picture window of some of the oldest vines in Dry Creek Valley. In addition to their Sauvignon Blanc and Zinfandel, another signature wine of Quivira's is known as Steelhead Red, formerly Dry Creek Cuvée. This Rhône-style blend of Grenache, Mourvèdre, Syrah, and Zinfandel was inspired by the old "field blends" that the Italian immigrants planted.

You can bring a picnic and sit out under the redwood and olive trees on the patio. Or if you prefer, in the tasting room there are board games like chess, Chinese checkers, backgammon, and solitaire to play during your visit. At Quivira, a leisurely stopover with extraordinary wines feels civilized and cultured, just like its namesake.

# Seghesio Family Vineyards

**Seghesio Family Vineyards**
14730 Grove Street
Healdsburg, CA 95448
866-734-4374; 707-433-3579
Fax: 707-433-8495
Website: seghesio.com
Email: seghesio@seghesio.com

Winemaker: Ted Seghesio
Winery owners: Seghesio family

**Access**
Location: From Highway 101 take
the Dry Creek Road exit east. Turn
right at the first stoplight onto
Grove Street. The winery is about
half a mile up on the left.

Hours open for visits and tastings:
10:00 A.M. – 5:00 P.M. daily,
except major holidays.

**Tastings and Tours**
Charge for tasting? No.

Appointment necessary for tour?
No tours.

Typical wines offered: Arneis, Pinot
Grigio; Barbera, Petite Sirah, Pinot
Noir, Sangiovese, vineyard-
designated Zinfandels; Omaggio,
a proprietary blend of Cabernet
Sauvignon and Sangiovese.

Sales of wine-related items? Yes,
including books, logo wear,
and more. ☞

Walking into the tasting room of Seghesio Family Vineyards makes you feel like part of the family. The staff are locals, and many family members do various jobs around the winery. Tables and bookshelves hold cookbooks and wine books, most with an Italian angle. In cold weather a fireplace crackles in the warmth of the golden stucco walls, where family photos and artifacts hang. Across the tasting bar a wall of windows showcases the barrel room, where you can see wines being racked or witness the quiet aging of Seghesio's renowned Zinfandel and other red varietals.

On one visit I arrived with my palate on fire after enjoying a deliciously spicy pecan chile chicken breast from the nearby Oakville Grocery in Healdsburg. Wondering if I would be able to taste at all, a sip of Arneis was recommended, and its fruity, acidic flavor put the heat out. Arneis translates to "little rascal," and I'm glad it has such a refreshing effect. From that sip I came to realize that Seghesio's varietals have enough nuance and style to satisfy many tastes. A spicy Barbera brings my taste buds back to life. And the Cortina Zinfandel has a natural affinity with chocolate.

The story of the Seghesio family is typical of the Italian immigrants who formed the backbone of Sonoma County's wine industry in the early days. Patriarch Edouardo Seghesio came from the Piedmont region of Italy in 1886. He worked in the old Italian Swiss Colony in Asti, where bulk wine was processed by workers like himself. As an indentured employee, he was contracted to work for three years and be paid a lump sum at the end. The original papers describing the arrangement hang on the tasting room wall.

Edouardo met his bride-to-be, Angela Dionisia Vasconi, at Asti. They were married in 1893, and in 1895 they purchased what is known as Chianti Station, the Seghesio family's home ranch. Today, their picturesque cupola-topped Victorian is still a focal point on the west side of Highway 101 between Geyserville and Cloverdale.

In 1910, the Seghesios planted their first Zinfandel grapes, the varietal they now specialize in. From 1902, when Edouardo's winery was completed, until 1983, Seghesio wines were produced for others and sold by the gallon. As the younger generations matured and the wine market in California changed, the decision was made to start their own Seghesio brand. Today one of Sonoma's oldest grape-growing families produces seventy-five thousand cases of premium Zinfandel, Pinot Noir, and Italian varietals. Their motto, "old vines, new generation," fits.

There is often a special event going on at Seghesio, which has an active program for its club members that includes such treats as a sausage-making party after harvest. The barrel room is open during events like Winter Wineland, and you'll meet Seghesios dishing up those homemade sausages, plus wild mushroom soup and maybe some pasta from a family recipe.

To extend the feeling of being part of the family, there are bocce balls in the tasting room. You are welcome to borrow them and head out to the bocce courts. A demonstration rose garden is on the way. It boasts old and new varieties, with names like Just Joey, Iceberg, and French Perfume (what an aroma!). On some days the beautiful Italian-style *forno* in the garden may be stoked and hot wood-fired pizza pulled out. You are welcome to bring your picnic anytime and sit under the giant redwood and fir trees next to the fountain, with the creamy stucco winery walls making it seem like a family home in Italy.

### Picnics and Programs

Picnic area open to the public? Yes, under the trees next to the rose garden and bocce courts.

Picnic ingredients sold in Tasting Room? No. Downtown Healdsburg, with excellent take-out at the Charcuterie, Oakville Grocery, and Downtown Bakery, is a few blocks away.

Special events or wine-related programs? Russian River Wine Road Winter Wineland in January; Russian River Wine Road Barrel Tasting in March; Passport in April; ZAP Celebration in July.

Wine Club: Centennial Club offers quarterly wine shipments, discounts, pre-release wine sales, limited and library wines, and member-only events.

# Simi Winery

**Simi Winery**
16275 Healdsburg Avenue
P.O. Box 407
Healdsburg, CA 95448
707-473-3231
Fax: 707-433-6253
Website: simiwinery.com
Email: information@simiwinery
.com

Winemaker: Steve Reeder
Winery owner: Franciscan Estates,
Fine Wine Division of Constellation
Brands

**Access**

Location: About 1 mile north of
Healdsburg. From Highway 101
north- or southbound take the Dry
Creek Road exit, turn to the east,
and turn left at the second light onto
Healdsburg Avenue. The winery is
on the left.

Hours open for visits and tastings:
10:00 A.M. – 5:00 P.M. daily,
except major holidays.

**Tastings and Tours**

Charge for tasting? Yes. $5 for 4
current release wines; $10 for 4
reserve and vineyard-designate
wines (individual tasting fees also
for reserve wines). Fees applied to
wine purchases.

Appointment necessary for tour?
No.

Tours: Guided tours $3, 11:00 A.M.
& 2:00 P.M. daily. (Under 21 no
charge.)

Typical wines offered: Chardonnay,
Pinot Gris, Sauvignon Blanc;
Cabernet Sauvignon, Merlot, Petite
Sirah, Pinot Noir, Shiraz, Zinfandel.

Sales of wine-related items? Yes,
including shirts, books, tableware,
books, and a huge selection of gift
items.

**Picnics and Programs**

Picnic area open to the public? Yes,
under the redwood trees.

The redwood trees in front of Simi Winery were planted by Isabelle Simi at the end of Prohibition. Today they symbolize the growth, endurance, and stature of this winery that was established by two brothers in 1876. Its continued success is due to the commitment to preserve its stature, from the time of Isabelle Simi through its subsequent owners.

The story of Isabelle Simi, the winery, and its cutting-edge winemaking techniques is told during one of the best tours in the wine country, which begins under the redwood trees. If you are particularly interested in winemaking, this is your tour. It can take over an hour, depending on the group's interest, and is a mini-course on the influence of the respected Zelma Long, the former winemaker, who retired in 1999.

After Giuseppe and Pietro Simi emigrated from Italy to California as young men, they started making wine in San Francisco with Sonoma grapes that were carried by wagon to Petaluma and barged across the Bay. In 1881 they decided to move closer to their source and bought an existing winery in Healdsburg. Soon, the Simis purchased this property on the north side of Healdsburg and built the stone cellar you see next to the railroad tracks. In 1904, just as the cellar was being completed, the brothers died unexpectedly.

Isabelle, the daughter of Giuseppe and the only heir, inherited the business. Only fourteen years old, she had already worked closely with her father in all aspects of the winery. Supported by an amenable staff and her own aplomb, she took charge. Later, during the fourteen years of Prohibition, Isabelle sold off the vineyards to save the wine still in the cellar and keep the winery intact. When Prohibition ended in 1933 she was forty-three.

Two years after planting the redwoods, Isabelle opened the first tasting room in California in a 25,000-gallon champagne barrel she had converted. The present tasting room, with its arched ceiling supported by barrel staves, was inspired by the original. In 1970 Isabelle retired and sold the winery to one of her growers. Subsequent owners have maintained the commitment to preserving Simi's historical significance as well as its high reputation for winemaking.

On the tour, after a little hike around the old winery, you come to the crush pad, where state-of-the art equipment first arrived under the management of another of the wine country's influential women, Zelma Long. Her influence is felt in the current winemaking team's attention to winemaking details and continual upgrading. A briefing on Chardonnay informs you that Simi was a leader in introducing whole cluster pressing. You'll learn how important it is to keep oxygen out of the wine, the difference between barrel and stainless-steel fermentation, why Simi believes in the blending of different lots, and about Chardonnay's one and a half years in the bottle before release.

Cabernet Sauvignon and other grapes for red wine are fermented with their skins in tanks with open tops. The point is to extract tannins, which are present in the grape skins, and which help the wine develop, just short of

Picnic ingredients sold in Tasting Room? No. Downtown Healdsburg is 2 minutes away, with Healdsburg Charcuterie, Downtown Bakery, Oakville Grocery, and more.

Special events or wine-related programs? Wine and cheese exploration (call for schedule); "From our Kitchen to Yours" monthly events throughout the year, including Winter Wineland and Russian River Wine Road Barrel Tasting.

Wine Club: Expressions of Terroir Wine Club includes 6 other wineries and a variety of membership options. See website or call tasting room.

the point where they overpower the fruit. To promote vigorous fermentation, a "trickle-over" sprayer circulates the wine over the cap of skins that rises to the top. In some wineries the cap is punched down by hand or stirred by machine. Here, in six-thousand-gallon tanks, a pipe in the middle of the tank sucks the wine up and releases it in a fine spray that trickles through the color-giving cap, letting it filter back through. The fermentation and pump-over take six to seven days.

After the examination of red-wine making, the rest of the tour is as scenic as it is informative. The top floor of the old winery building is stacked with barrels. The Cabernet you witnessed in fermentation is aged in oak barrels like these. While in the barrels, the wine is occasionally racked. This is done by inserting a hose in the middle of the barrel to remove the wine without disturb-

ing the lees, or fruit residue, that settles to the bottom. If left in the wine the lees will leave it cloudy, making it look like a bottle of unfiltered apple juice.

A trek down the stairs brings you to more barrels and the original winery with its three-foot-thick stone walls. It was here that Isabelle stored the wine during Prohibition. When it was over, she had inventory ready to go, while other wineries had to restart from scratch.

Although many relics from the original winery are being replaced, the juxtaposition of old and new remains as you first see it through the redwoods across the railroad tracks. Most days, barrels are being cleaned or stored on the covered porch of the picturesque stone winery. That won't change. And neither will the long-lasting reputation of Simi wines.

# Trentadue Winery

**Trentadue Winery**
19170 Geyserville Avenue
Geyserville, CA 95441
707-433-3104
Fax: 707-433-5825
Website: trentadue.com
Email: info@trentadue.com

Winemaker: Miro Tcholakov
Winery owners: Leo and Evelyn
Trentadue

**Access**

Location: About 5 miles north of
Healdsburg. From Highway 101
north- or southbound take the
Independence Lane exit east, and
head north on Geyserville Avenue.
The winery gates with the lions are
on the right.

Hours open for visits and tastings:
10:00 A.M – 5:00 P.M daily, except
major holidays.

**Tastings and Tours**

Charge for tasting? Not for basic
list. Reserve La Storia wines and
Ports, $5 for a flight. Port &
Chocolate Pairing, $10, includes
logo port glass.

Appointment necessary for tour?
Yes.

Tours: Gondola Tour of vineyard for
minimum of 8 people, $15 each.

Typical wines offered: Sparkling
Wine; Sauvignon Blanc, Viognier;
Cabernet Sauvignon, 

In the heat of summer, the tree-shaded driveway and the sprawling oaks, redwoods, and arbors around Trentadue Winery provide a cooling respite. Surrounded by vineyards on the floor of Alexander Valley, Trentadue has some enticing programs for visitors. But first you might like to know *la storia*, which is Italian for the history. It is also the name of the Trentadue event room two stories above the tasting bar and of their line of high-end wines.

Trentadue's founders, Leo and Evelyn Trentadue (pronounced *tren-ta-doo* by the family), began cultivating grapes in the middle of Alexander Valley in 1959. Ten years later, after growing grapes for other wineries, the Trentadues decided to make wine. When they bought the 250 acres just south of Geyserville, the property included Carignane and Merlot vines that were already more than seventy years old. They planted Zinfandel, Merlot, Sangiovese, Petite Sirah, and more. Some of the old vines are still here.

One of the best ways to learn more about the vineyards is to grab seven of your friends and arrange to take the Gondola Tour. Seeing the historic property in the middle of this beautiful valley is not only informative, but also a sensory exploration. Climb aboard the gondola with its bench and bucket seats, and you'll be pulled by one of the winery tractors and make a loop through the vineyard. First stop is the magnificent old Carignane vines, all the more imposing because of their shape. These "head pruned" vines stand alone, which is the way the old-timers pruned, in contrast to the other pruning and trellising techniques you'll see in the newer vineyards. In the summer you can taste the grapes along the way.

Another sight is the triangular block near the parking lot, where the young vines in Trentadue's "Adopt a Vine" program grow. While anyone can adopt one of these Zinfandel or Petite Sirah vines, with the many weddings that take place at Trentadue, the staff wanted something memorable to "tie" the bride and groom to the place. Each vine is tagged with a metal plaque engraved with the name of the "parents" and the date it was adopted.

The tour finishes in the tasting room. Here you'll learn that Trentadue is Italian for "32," which explains why Cuvee 32 is the name of their Super Tuscan style blend on the new La Storia line of wines, packaged in iridescent bottles complete with real gold in the etched label. Super Tuscan refers to the Sangiovese-based wines from Tuscany that include such French varietals as Merlot and Cabernet Sauvignon. You can begin the tasting with Trentadue's refreshing sparkling wine, or have a sip of Sauvignon Blanc or Viognier, but what this winery is known for are the reds. Old Patch is still on the tasting menu, as are Zinfandel, Merlot, Cabernet Sauvignon and La Storia Zinfandel, Cuvee 32, and Meritage, a blend of Bordeaux varietals, all made from grapes grown by the Trentadue family in Alexander Valley and at a family vineyard in Dry Creek Valley.

Next come Trentadue's Ports. To show them off, Trentadue offers a Port and Chocolate Pairing complete with tasting sheet and an international selection of chocolates to go with the Viognier, Zinfandel, Petite Sirah Ports, and the one-of-a-kind Chocolate Amore. The last one, which is a Merlot-based Port, is blended with chocolate essence just before bottling. Served in a chocolate cup made especially for Trentadue by Gravenstein Chocolate Company in Santa Rosa, this dessert-in-a-glass has a natural tasting finish of chocolate, balanced by the bittersweet richness of Port.

Cheese, crackers, and a variety of condiments are sold in the tasting room, or you can bring your own basket of cold cuts and bread to go with the hearty and fruit-rich Italian-style wines. Although the beautiful grounds are sometimes reserved for weddings or company picnics, the Trentadues always welcome bike riders and other wine-tasting picnickers to their oasis in the middle of the vines. To open a picnic basket under the cooling shade of the grapevine-covered arbor or on a table next to the Tuscan-style tasting room is to indulge in relaxation Italian-style. The surrounding vineyards, the fountains, and the cooling arbor are reminders of the influence of generations of Italians like the Trentadues who have embraced this valley.

Carignane, Merlot, Pinot Noir, Petite Sirah, Sangiovese, Zinfandel; varietal Ports from Merlot, Petite Sirah, Viognier, Zinfandel.

Sales of wine-related items? Yes, including picnic items, giftware, and shirts.

**Picnics and Programs**
Picnic area open to the public? Yes, under the arbor or next to the visitor's center. Venues including the Sala del Leone available to rent for weddings and other events.

Picnic ingredients sold in Tasting Room? Yes, including Sonoma Jack cheese, salami, crackers, estate olive oil, and fresh bread on weekends.

Special events or wine-related programs? Russian River Wine Road Winter Wineland in January; Russian River Wine Road Barrel Tasting in March; Taste of the Valley in June; Food and Wine Affair in November; Festival of Lights in December. Weddings and other events accommodated in Sala del Leone, and smaller groups for lunches and tastings in La Storia.

Wine Club: The "32" Wine Club and the "32" Port Club offer wine shipments, tasting-room discounts, and special events.

# Western
# Sonoma County

# Foppiano Vineyards

Foppiano Vineyards
12707 Old Redwood Highway
P.O. Box 606
Healdsburg, CA 95448
707-433-7272
Fax: 707-433-0565
Website: foppiano.com
Email: lfoppiano@foppiano.com

Winemaker: Bill Regan
Winery owner: Louis J. Foppiano

## Access

Location: About 2 miles south of Healdsburg. From Highway 101 northbound, take the Healdsburg Avenue exit and turn left; from Highway 101 southbound take the Old Redwood Highway exit and turn right. Winery is about half a mile up on the right. Watch for the sign.

Hours open for visits and tastings: 10 A.M. – 4:30 P.M. daily, except major holidays.

## Tastings and Tours

Charge for tasting? No.

Appointment necessary for tour? No.

Tours: Self-guided vineyard tour any time. Pick up brochure in the tasting room.

Typical wines offered: Chardonnay, Sauvignon Blanc; Cabernet Sauvignon, Merlot, Petite Sirah, Sangiovese, Zinfandel.

The history of a family and its wine attracts visitors to Foppiano. If it weren't for the roadside sign pointing the way, you might drive past this serviceable beige winery on Old Redwood Highway that resembles a warehouse. This is Petite Sirah territory, as you'll soon see.

Drive in slowly and park by the retired Northwestern Pacific railcar or the winery. Stretched out between you and the Russian River are the vineyards of Sonoma County's oldest family-owned winery.

Inside the tasting room decorated with family photos and wine awards, the staff, led by Susan Foppiano-Valera, pours wine, recommends the self-guided vineyard tour, and shares the winery's story. Ask them to relate this saga that parallels Italian-American winemaking in northern California before everyone was named Louis.

The first Foppiano was Giovanni, an Italian immigrant lured to California by the Gold Rush in 1864. When that didn't pan out he settled near Healdsburg and started farming fruits and vegetables. Thirty-two years and ten children later he purchased this ranch with a working winery adjacent to the Russian River.

In 1896 Foppiano produced his first wine, a blend based on Petite Sirah, the grape that has become the winery's standard bearer. Giovanni's son, Louis A., then nineteen, sold the wine in barrels to fellow Italian Americans in San Francisco's North Beach neighborhood. Louis A. eventually finagled a way to purchase the winery for himself and his wife in 1910, which led to a grudgeful silence between father and son that lasted until just before Giovanni's death.

Meanwhile Louis A. developed and marketed Foppiano wines and built a reputation for good value from coast to coast. But Prohibition in 1919, followed by the Great Depression ten years later, brought the business to a standstill. A photo in the tasting room shows the dumping of the wine along the roadside while a federal revenuer stands by. Louis A. went back to farming fruits and vegetables and grapes for the table. He died in 1924.

His son Louis J., born in 1910, eventually took charge. He rebuilt the winery in 1937 and constructed one of the first bottling lines at that time in California. A 1940 tasting-room photo shows one of the five to six wine-filled tank cars that made weekly trips to New York when World War II cut off European wine.

In 1966, recognizing America's growing interest in premium California wine, the Foppianos began to focus on varietals in addition to their popular jug wines. They replanted apple and prune orchards with Cabernet Sauvignon, Merlot, and Chardonnay. Old Petite Sirah vines remain, and their gnarled thick trunks are a highlight on the vineyard tour.

After hearing the history of the family, take a glass of wine along if you like (just be sure to return the glass), and pick up the brochure for the self-guided walking tour of the vineyard. The sights along this gentle leg-stretch change from week to week as the vines bud, leaf, bear fruit, and are harvested and pruned.

The tour begins with Foppiano's trademark Petite Sirah vines and a description of the grape's heritage. Recent studies using DNA confirm that Petite Sirah originated when a French nurseryman, Dr. Durif, crossed Syrah with Peloursin in the nineteenth century. You'll see old and new Petite Sirah vines as you continue. The third stop is at a wind generator, which is used with a heating system for frost protection. The silt pond is next, and then it's on to the Cabernet Sauvignon and Chardonnay blocks, where you'll learn a bit about how they are grown, their age, and potentials. A stop at the Vineyard Vista allows a brief presentation on the cooling effects provided by the Russian River's pathway to the ocean. Fog comes up the river in the summer. Fewer hours of sunshine and more rain than other areas of Sonoma County create the right combination for growing the varietals planted here—including Merlot and Cabernet Sauvignon.

In the spring you can expect a demonstration of thinning. If you tour during harvest, a wild time to visit, you'll get to watch the grapes being cut off the vine and transported into the winery. Have a taste of a perfectly ripe Petite Sirah grape, then head back into the tasting room.

Rich, tannic, and full-flavored, Petite Sirah has been the darling of the Foppianos since the first vintage in 1896. As Lou Foppiano says, "We plan to keep making Petite Sirah until our teeth turn purple."

Sales of wine-related items? Yes, including books and logo clothing.

## Picnics and Programs
Picnic area open to the public? Yes, under the walnut tree outside the tasting room.

Picnic ingredients sold in Tasting Room? No. Pick up ingredients in Healdsburg at Oakville Grocery, Downtown Bakery, or Healdsburg Charcuterie.

Special events or wine-related programs? Russian River Wine Road Winter Wineland in January; Russian River Wine Road Barrel Tasting in March; Fall Open House. See website for more.

Wine Club: 1896 Society includes quarterly wine shipments, discounts on wine and gift items, and an annual party.

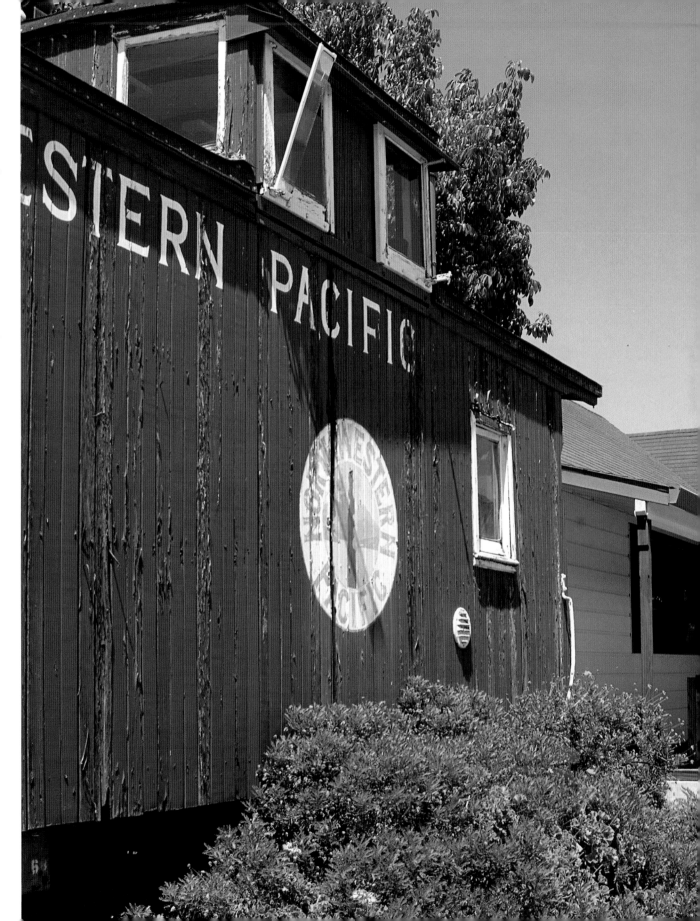

# Hop Kiln Winery

Hop Kiln Winery
6050 Westside Road
Healdsburg, CA 95448
707-433-6491
Fax: 707-433-8162
Website: hopkilnwinery.com
Email: info@hopkilnwinery.com

Winemaker: Steve Strobl
Winery owner: Westside Grapes
LLC, Seattle; David diLoreto,
executive director

**Access**
Location: About 6 miles southwest
of Healdsburg. From Highway 101
northbound take the Healdsburg
Downtown exit; from Highway 101
southbound take the Westside Road
exit. Head west on Mill Street,
which turns into Westside Road.
Proceed approximately 6 miles to
the winery.

Hours open for visits and tastings:
10:00 A.M. – 5:00 P.M. daily,
except major holidays.

**Tastings and Tours**
Charge for tasting? No.

Appointment necessary for tour?
No tour.

Typical wines offered: Chardonnay,
Gewürztraminer, Riesling; A
Thousand Flowers fruity white
blend; Cabernet Sauvignon, Pinot
Noir, Valdiguié, three estate

Whether you're rounding the S-turn on Westside Road by bicycle or car, California Historical Landmark 893 irresistibly draws your attention. On a bank high over the Russian River, the triple turrets of the old kiln ventilators and the triangular roofs topping the stone-and-timber building make this one of the most intriguing winery settings in Sonoma County.

Dr. Martin Griffin had that sense about the dilapidated hop kiln in 1960 when he purchased it as part of a 240-acre sheep ranch. Built in 1905 to dry hops that were turned into beer, the kiln was in use until the early 1940s. The vineyards you see stretched out across the floodplain and rolling hillsides are on the old hop fields. When hops were wiped out by downy mildew, the blight shut down the industry in Sonoma County. The only hops left here are the ones you see climbing up the façade of the building each year.

As you approach the magnificent structure, look closely at the meticulous restoration of the stonework originally built by Angelo "Skinny" Sodini, a stonemason who also worked on Jack London's Wolf House. Around the side is the rustic redwood winery and tasting room, once a storage facility for the hops. Up a few stairs and through the heavy redwood door, you may have to pause while your eyes adjust to the darkness of the aged-redwood interior.

There is plenty to see from the overlook in the tasting room. If you stretch your neck you should be able to see the arched stone doors that lead into what were once kilns. Today, stacks of barrels and bottles of aging wine fill the old fireboxes. Above the wine are slatted wood "nets," which held loads of hop flowers that were dried when the kiln was fired. A maze of pipes ran through the towers to carry out the smoke. Each tower opened and closed to regulate the heat. The toasted dry hops were stored where the tasting room is, then baled and shipped to breweries.

Where barrels now fill the bottom floor, an old track used to carry a small railcar that transported the toasted hops out of the kiln. A hop display on the wall shows more about how this building was used.

All the grapes for the eight to ten thousand cases of wines are grown here at the Griffin Vineyard. Microclimates, specific pockets of heat, fog, sun, or shade, favor different varietals. Although the Russian River appellation is known for its cool nights and foggy summer mornings, slight variations within the climate enable different varietals to thrive on the same ranch. The sunny hillsides, reminiscent of Provence, are where Petite Sirah, Zinfandel, and the Rhône varietal Valdiguié grow best. A cooler area comparable to the Rhine Valley in Germany supports Johannisberg Riesling grapes.

In addition to the hop exhibit, newspaper clippings on the walls commemorate the films that have been made at the winery. And contemporary art exhibitions change every six weeks.

Whether two or twenty people are in the tasting room, their elbows on the bar, the banter is always lively and flows in multiple directions. For example, you'll find out that this small hands-on winery produces less than ten thousand cases of wine a year, and all the wine is grown on this estate. You may also hear that the pond is a bird sanctuary and is surrounded by all-native plants. Lovers of horticulture will be glad to know that many of the shrubs, trees, and flowers around the grounds have little labels identifying them.

You can take a bottle of Marty's Big Red or perhaps the refreshing Thousand Flowers blend of Gewürztraminer and Riesling outside to the picnic area. Under the magnificent fig tree that was planted in 1880, you're likely to share the space with bicyclers, who've made this a popular stop while touring the area.

Zinfandels, Marty's Big Red; late-harvest Zinfandel.

Sales of wine-related items? Yes, logo glasses, hats, aprons, shirts, and napkins.

**Picnics and Programs**
Picnic area open to the public? Yes.

Picnic ingredients sold in Tasting Room? Yes, including Sonoma cheese, salami, and crackers.

Special events or wine-related programs? Russian River Wine Road Winter Wineland, Russian River Wine Road Road Barrel Tasting.

Wine Club: Hop Kiln Wine Club includes quarterly wine shipments, discounts and special prices, and annual dinner.

# Iron Horse Vineyards

Iron Horse Vineyards
9786 Ross Station Road
Sebastopol, CA 95472
707-887-1507
Fax: 707-887-1337
Website: ironhorsevineyards.com
Email: info@ironhorsevineyards
.com

Winemakers: Forrest Tancer and
Dave Munksgard
Winery owners: Barry and Audrey
Sterling, Joy Sterling and Forrest
Tancer, Laurence Sterling

## Access
Location: About 12 miles west of
Santa Rosa. From Highway 101
take the Steele Lane/Guerneville
Road exit, and turn west; this turns
into Guerneville Road. Take it to the
end, turn right on Highway 116
(Gravenstein Highway), and in
about 1 mile, at Kozlowski Farms,
turn left on Ross Station Road, continuing 1 mile to the stone-framed
gate with an iron horse on each side.

Hours open for visits and tastings:
10:30 A.M. – 3:30 P.M. daily,
except major holidays.

## Tastings and Tours
Charge for tasting? Yes. $5, applied
to purchase.

Appointment necessary for tour?
Yes.

Tours: By appointment.

The first glimpse of Iron Horse from the facing slope on Ross Station Road is a vision. The diamond-shaped hill is cut by emerald vines in summer and chains of coppery leaves in autumn. Winding up to the pinnacle, a sentry of palm and olive trees (yes, it's been called Palmolive Way) lines the last stretch to the parking lot.

The tiny tasting room is in the farthest of the barn-red buildings at the north end of the knoll. The informality and simplicity of the structures give the winery the appearance of a working farm, nothing as fancy as the reputation of the owners would portend.

The view, on the other hand, is something to behold. On a clear day you can see all the way across Sonoma County to Napa's Mount St. Helena. Turn around, and in the summer the fog may be just rolling in from or creeping back to the Pacific, only twelve miles away. It is this proximity to the ocean and the resultant extra coolness that established "Green Valley" as its own appellation in the Russian River region.

In good weather the tasting bar is outside. If you've made an appointment for a tour, you'll be offered a glass of sparkling wine while a brief history of the winery is shared. The Iron Horse name comes from the train—a spur of the Petaluma–Russian River line—that used to stop at Ross Station.

Barry and Audrey Sterling purchased the property in 1976. His occupation as an international attorney and hers as hostess and restoration expert had kept them on the go for over twenty years. The ranch offered them a place to settle down and realize Barry's dream of gardening, raising grapes, and making wine. The hundred-year-old Carpenter Gothic farmhouse where they now live challenged Audrey's restoration skills, but was worth the effort.

Barry's son Laurence and his family, and his daughter Joy and her husband Forrest Tancer, also live at the ranch. Forrest helped develop the initial vineyards on the property and is the winemaker as well as a partner in Iron Horse. Joy is the marketing manager and travels frequently promoting Iron Horse wines. She has authored four books about various aspects of her life in viticulture: *A Cultivated Life, Vintage Feasting, Vineyard: A Year in the Life of California Wine Country,* and *A Vintner's Guide to Red Wine.*

For the tour, with flute in hand, you take a trip down the hill to the riddling cellar. Here thousands of bottles, in mechanized and manual riddling racks, are turned twice a day in their final stages of secondary fermentation. A good hand riddler can turn two thousand cases in a couple of hours. Technically, it takes only two weeks for bubbles to develop in sparkling wine, but the bottles here are left on the yeast for more than three years. The longer time produces a more complex and sophisticated *méthode champenoise* sparkler. The bouquet, which refers to the wine's more yeasty aroma, intensifies. The longer time on the yeast also produces a creamier texture. And the finish develops a perception of sweetness that comes from the fruit, not from sugar. The wine is stored in heavy plywood bins known as gyros that hold 488 bottles and are earthquake-proof.

As you head back to the winery you pass the redwood building that houses the laboratory. Above it are two presses, one for sparkling wine and one for still. Up the grassy hill is an arbored picnic area, one of Iron Horse's entertaining spots, where you can feast on the Sterlings' view. The hill to the northwest is topped with Pinot Noir grapes. In certain vintages the grapes are so

Typical wines offered: Brut, Brut Rosé, Blanc de Blancs, Wedding Cuvée (Blanc de Noirs); Russian Cuvee and Brut LD (late disgorged) sparkling wines; Chardonnay, Sauvignon Blanc, Viognier; Cabernet Sauvignon, Pinot Noir.

Sales of wine-related items? No.

**Picnics and Programs**
Picnic area open to the public? No.

Picnic ingredients sold in Tasting Room? No.

Special events or wine-related programs? Call for schedule or check website.

Wine Club: Iron Horse Corral Club offers wine shipments of limited releases, special discounts, and exclusive winery events.

wonderful they become part of a *tête de cuvée*, a top-of-the-line sparkling wine that stays on the yeast for at least four years. The top of the line becomes Iron Horse's Brut LD, a late-disgorged limited release.

If Forrest Tancer happens by, ask him about his pride, the vineyard. He'll tell you about the soil type, which is known as Gold Ridge, "a sandy soil that, so far, phylloxera doesn't like." On the 330-acre ranch, 180 are planted in grapes. The huge riparian corridor that surrounds the ranch, including 30 acres of wild blackberries and 8 acres of fruit and vegetable gardens, illustrates the principle that avoiding a monoculture is a protection against phylloxera.

Barry Sterling's passion is the gardens that feed both the families on the ranch and the guests at their many parties. Even in winter, when lettuce, leeks, and artichokes are all that grow, vegetables are always being harvested. In the summer, the big garden at the entrance is a mouth-watering showpiece, with forty-two kinds of tomatoes, as many peppers and chiles, and six kinds of basil. In October, a grand finale showcases hundreds of pumpkins dotting the floodplain around the bridge. Visitors are asked to come up to the winery and check in before walking around the gardens.

Return to the tasting bar, backlit by the afternoon sun, for the priceless view and the practical setting that reflect the way the owners want you to think of their wine: "sophisticated, friendly, and easy to drink."

# J Vineyards & Winery

J Vineyards & Winery
11447 Old Redwood Highway
Healdsburg, CA 95448
707-431-3646
Fax: 707-431-5410
Website: jwine.com
Email: winefolk@jwine.com

Winemaker: Oded Shakked
Winery owner: Judy Jordan

**Access**

Location: About 2½ miles south of Healdsburg. From Highway 101 northbound take the Healdsburg Avenue exit and turn left; from Highway 101 southbound take the Old Redwood Highway exit and turn right. Winery is in about 1½ miles on the right and shares an entrance with Rodney Strong Vineyards.

Hours open for visits and tastings: 11:00 A.M. – 5:00 P.M. daily, except major holidays.

**Tastings and Tours**

Charge for tasting? Yes. Wine & Food Pairing Flights, $10 at the bar daily with "add on" specials; $20 – $25 in the Bubble Room Friday – Sunday; single food with one wine available for $5. Groups of 10 should call ahead for reservations.

Appointment necessary for tour? No tour.

Typical wines offered: *Méthode champenoise* vintage Brut and other sparkling wine; Chardonnay; Pinot Noir; and offerings of limited special varietals. ☞

No other winery opened its doors with a food and wine program like J did when the tasting room made its debut in 1999. Putting her money where her mouth was, owner Judy Jordan wanted to show how her signature *méthode champenoise* sparkling wine and J's other varietals taste with creative and compatible appetizers.

While the avant-garde interior of the tasting room evokes a cool, modern formality, the gregarious staff and the delicious tastings make this one of the best stops in the wine country. Whether you go for the stand-up tasting at the bar or sit down in the Bubble Room, having a bite to eat is a welcome interval, especially if you are trying to cover more than a couple of wineries in a day. And while everyone seems to be talking about putting food with their wine, here it is an informative experience, done with a lot of class that isn't intimidating or stuffy. I always learn something here about balance and flavors.

While the menus change regularly, a sampling might begin with Vintage Brut and a spear of endive topped with ginger-lime Dungeness crab salad. I found Chardonnay matched a cool sip of vichyssoise topped with red tobikko and a dash of chive oil. Then came Pinot Noir next to a mini-roulade of prosciutto, cherry confit, and mascarpone cheese on crostini. Flavors of salt, sweet, tart, and cheesy interplayed deliciously with the dusty berry components in the Pinot. And the *coup de grâce* was a savory strudellette filled with Parmesan and wild mushrooms, redolent of porcini and paired with a five-year-old Pinot Noir. The sampling was served in four bites on a celadon Japanese-style sushi plate with the wines in their appropriate shaped glasses lined up on the bar.

For the sit-down menu served in the Bubble Room, the portions are slightly larger and the wines are older vintages and reserves. In this most civilized setting, whether you are sunk into the long, cozy couches with your tasting on the coffee table, or in comfortable upholstered chairs at the polished wood table, you'll find this tasting is a destination, a place to meet friends, and educational to boot. The light-filled room with its view of the garden and "moat" only adds to the experience.

Attention to detail is so important here that the Champagne glasses are specially made for J. The glasses have an etched scoring inside on the bottom to enhance the bubble movement. The result is a geyser of millions of tiny starlike bubbles.

The staff will tell you that their wines come from a cool growing region in the Russian River, and food is easy to pair with them. Nonetheless, the resident chef has a knack for making every bite have enough going on to satisfy many palates. "When you taste a wine by itself and then take it home and have it with dinner, it can taste differently," says the staff. "Tasting wine with food opens up its potential."

Judy Jordan started making *méthode champenoise* sparkling wine in 1987. She founded J Vineyards & Winery at the time with her father, Tom Jordan, the proprietor of Jordan Winery on the other side of Healdsburg. When the old Piper Sonoma winery became available, Judy moved her brand and initiated the remodeling project, a one-of-a-kind architectural statement.

J, in the same cul-de-sac as Rodney Strong Vineyards, has attracted a groupie following. If you go to one of the Russian River Wine Road events such as the Winter Wineland, you'll find a line waiting to get in and a crowd here throughout the day. During events, the food and wine pairings are set up on the walkway upstairs. From this landing above the winery, you can view the bottling line on one side and the riddling on the other. In automatic riddlers, 578 bottles are rotated in each bin to remove the spent Champagne yeast cells, a process that takes up to three weeks.

While you enjoy the tasting menu, there is plenty to talk about in the tasting room. The bar and the wall behind it are made from cold rolled steel that is acid washed, giving it a patina in the bluish light. A fiber-optic line behind four-inch glass panes in the wall creates an icy blue glow. High ceilings and a domed skylight add an airiness to the room, in which wine is the major item for purchase. But you can also get some bubbles for blowing contained in a miniature J bottle to wear around your neck, an attractive bottle of J champagne vinegar, and a tasteful selection of shirts, leather wine carriers, and cookbooks.

As you depart and cross the bridge, with the flower-rimmed moat underneath, I suspect you'll be hooked on J. It's a place that beckons your return.

Sales of wine-related items? Yes, including logo outerwear and polo shirts, leather wine carriers, logo wine glasses, corkscrews, flavored olive oils, J champagne vinegar, and cookbooks.

**Picnics and Programs**
Picnic area open to the public? No.

Picnic ingredients sold in Tasting Room? No.

Special events or wine-related programs? Russian River Wine Road Winter Wineland in January; Russian River Wine Road Barrel Tasting in March; Russian River Vintners & Winegrowers Grape to Glass in August and Wine & Food Affair in November; Sparkling Holidays at the end of November – December.

Wine Club: Club J membership includes quarterly wine shipments, complimentary wine and food pairings; discount in the Bubble Room tasting, private tours, wine discounts, and member-only events.

# Korbel Champagne Cellars

**Korbel Champagne Cellars**
13250 River Road
Guerneville, CA 95446
707-824-7317
Fax: 707-869-2506
Website: korbel.com
Email: info@korbel.com

Winemaker: Paul Ahvenianen
Winery owner: Gary Heck

### Access

Location: About 16 miles west of Santa Rosa, 5 miles east of Guerneville. From Highway 101 take the River Road exit and proceed 12 miles. The winery is on the right.

Hours open for visits and tastings: Tasting Room and Delicatessen & Market: 9:00 A.M – 5:00 P.M. daily, except major holidays.

### Tastings and Tours

Charge for tasting? No.

Appointment necessary for tour? No.

Tours: Historic winery tours 10:00 A.M. – 3:00 P.M daily.

Garden tours: Tuesday – Sunday: 11:00 A.M., 1:00 P.M. & 3:00 P.M.

Typical wines offered for tasting: Blanc de Blancs, Blanc de Noirs, Brut, Brut Rosé, Extra Dry, Natural, Sec sparkling wines; Chardonnay; Cabernet Sauvignon, Pinot Noir, Zinfandel; Port; Cream Sherry. Brandy available for sale, not tasting.

Sales of wine-related items? Yes, glasses, corks, books, corkscrews, novelty items, dishes, linens, and logo clothing.

### Picnics and Programs

Picnic area open to the public? Yes.

Picnic ingredients sold in Tasting Room? Adjacent is the Korbel Delicatessen and Market, with complete hot and cold deli entrées and daily specials, packaged foods, and more.

Special events or wine-related programs? Russian River Wine Road Winter Wineland in January; ☞

Korbel's historic ivy-covered winery houses a museum of early California winemaking. Stately among the second-growth redwoods, the imposing façade overlooks Pinot Noir and Chardonnay vineyards along a narrow bend of the Russian River, only fifteen miles from the coast.

Hourly tours begin at the old train depot, once a stop for the Northwestern Pacific Railway that between 1876 and 1935 brought vacationers and supplies from San Francisco to Russian River hamlets. Inside the yellow clapboard depot you can view antique photos featuring the Korbel brothers Francis, Anton, and Joseph; the winery's first Champagne master, Frank Hasek; trays of fruit drying where grapes now grow; and a rare snowfall in 1890.

The tour guides are as much docents as wine experts as they dispense their wealth of biographical—and sometimes juicy—tidbits about the winery and its proprietors. The first and most photogenic stop on the tour, a round brick tower set behind the winery, houses a thirty-three-foot vertical pot still. Its significance is the starting point for the Korbel story and that of other immigrants who came in search of the American dream.

In the mid-1800s the three Korbel brothers came to California as political refugees from Bohemia, now the Czech Republic. Their defiance of the Hapsburgs had landed the oldest brother in prison, from which he escaped. The brandy tower, a replica of his prison turret, was built as a reminder of the political persecution that he had endured and they had fled.

Stepping into the old winery through painted redwood doors you pass a collection of barrels and ancient farm equipment. A few stairs lead down to one of the original cellars, saved from a fire when a quick-thinking worker pulled the bungs out of barrels on the floor above and let out the wine.

Along the wall, photographs and memorabilia chronicle the family's enterprises. In 1862, when the Korbels arrived in San Francisco, they manufactured cigar boxes and ornate house trim from redwood. The redwood groves along the Russian River first attracted the Korbels to the area. After logging the property, they raised prune plums, wheat, corn, alfalfa, tobacco, and grapes. Finding grapes to be the most profitable, they started making wine in 1882.

The success of one grape they had planted, the Black Pinot, or Pinot Noir, suggested that varietal's specialty—Champagne—as an option. By the mid-1890s Korbel Champagne was launched, and except for the years of Prohibition, production has been continuous.

From tidbits thrown in with the winery history, you'll learn that the brothers didn't marry until they were in their thirties and forties, when their mother sent three Czech girls to be their brides. Fifteen children came from the three couples.

After the oldest Korbel retired to Europe and the other two died, the inheritance-sharing cousins ran through the family fortune in a generation and sold the winery to Adolf Heck in 1954, seventy-two years after it was founded.

Heck incorporated his ideas for making a "California-style" champagne that showcases dry, fruity

Russian River Wine Road Barrel Tasting in March; Mother's Day Wine & Roses; Father's Day Pops & Corks; and monthly events. See website for more.

Wine Club: Korbel Wine Club offers discounts on wine, access to limited releases, and tasting room – only products.

flavors over the previous yeasty European style. Korbel Brut, released in 1956, is the result, and Korbel Natural updated the bubbly to an even more sophisticated palate. It is one of thirteen sparkling wines included in the over 1.2 million plus cases sold annually. Adolf's son Gary now runs the winery. Korbel now produces still wines and four hundred thousand cases of brandy. Heck also owns Lake Sonoma Winery in Dry Creek Valley, Kenwood Vineyards, and Valley of the Moon in Sonoma Valley.

The specifics of winemaking are featured on the rest of the tour, first with a short film. Next, a walk-through takes you past riddling, dosaging, and corking demonstrations. You'll see the automatic riddling machine that Adolf Heck invented in 1966, and finally a display of Korbel antiquities including the world's largest crystal Champagne glass and a thirty-two-gallon Champagne bottle that weighs four hundred pounds and can serve six hundred to a thousand people. The winery tour ends under the redwoods outside the tasting room.

The garden tour showcases a more feminine side of the historic property. With the Korbels' Czech brides came plant seeds, some of which continue to grow around the old family home, built in 1874. In addition to more than 250 roses, you'll see asters and Chinese lanterns, variegated hydrangea, pineapple lilies, the original crepe myrtles, honeysuckles, and a loquat tree that came from Luther Burbank.

From the garden, visits to the tasting room with its emporium of merchandise is one stop, and the other is for lunch in the Delicatessen and Market, where outside seating is conducive to lingering. In case you wonder where all the wine is made, if you look to the right on your way out of the parking lot, you can catch a glimpse of Korbel's high-tech winery, in high contrast with your visit to the archives of the past.

# Rodney Strong Vineyards

Rodney Strong Vineyards
11455 Old Redwood Highway
Healdsburg, CA 95448
866-779-4637; 707-431-1533
Fax: 707-433-8635
Website: rodneystrong.com
Email: info@rodneystrong.com

Winemaker: Rick Sayre
Winery owner: Klein Family Vintners

**Access**
Location: About 2½ miles south of
Healdsburg. From Highway 101
northbound take the Healdsburg
Avenue exit and turn left; heading
south take the Old Redwood
Highway exit and turn right. The
winery is in about 1½ miles on the
right, and shares an entrance with
J Vineyards & Winery.

Hours open for visits and tastings:
10:00 A.M. – 5:00 P.M. daily,
except major holidays.

**Tastings and Tours**
Charge for tasting? No.

Appointment necessary for tour?
No.

Tours: 11:00 A.M. & 3:00 P.M.
daily. No charge.

Typical wines offered: Chardonnay,
Sauvignon Blanc; Cabernet
Sauvignon, Pinot Noir, Merlot,
Zinfandel. ☞

When you pull into the parking lot just off Old Redwood Highway between Windsor and Healdsburg, the pyramid shape and well-kept grounds allude to the prevailing success of this quintessential Sonoma County winery. Founded in 1959 by its namesake, Rodney Strong Vineyards was purchased by the Klein family in 1989. All wine continues to be made from Sonoma County grapes. A thousand acres of Sonoma vineyards are now owned by the winery, which produces around five hundred thousand cases of wine annually.

The layered building was designed by Craig Rowland, an understudy of Frank Lloyd Wright. If you go up the stairs and into the building you'll find the interior chamber that serves as the tasting room. Around it, the winery was built with four wings in the shape of a cross as an efficiency experiment, and it works. Designed to make use of the central space under the tasting room, the winery can economically move an enormous amount of wine from one area of the winery to another for filtering, aging, or bottling. Fermentation, storage, and barrel rooms stretch out below the railing in hundred-foot-long spokes.

You can take a self-guided Wine Gallery Tour around the perimeter of the tasting room or, if you prefer, a guided tour is offered twice a day.

Equally interesting are the historic and viticultural displays and exhibits on the walls and doorways. Begin counterclockwise to follow the chronological story from the days when Rodney Strong planted the first Pinot Noir on this estate in 1968. You can still see those delicious vines adjacent to the winery on the other side of the "Green," which is used for summer concerts and picnics. This vineyard is next to the east fork of the Russian River, where the coastal climate of cool nights and hot days is conducive to Pinot Noir. The grapes for the winery's acclaimed Cabernet Sauvignon are grown in Alexander Valley, where the heat is more intense. With vineyards in Alexander Valley, Russian River Valley, and Chalk Hill, this is a good place to taste wines that are made from grapes particularly suited to their site.

A favorite part of the visit is the old Zinfandel vine on display. This close-up shows the size and beauty of the gnarled vine, whose shape comes from old-fashioned "head pruning." In the spring, when the vines sprout new growth, they resemble the head of Medusa. While most grapes planted today have some sort of trellis to hold the vines and help with canopy management as well as ripening and then harvesting, the older vines continue to be head pruned. Grapevines are considered old when they are at least thirty, when they begin to lose 10 to 12 percent of production each year. At the same time the fruit becomes more intensely flavored, which is why vintners prize the old-growth fruit.

In one spoke of the winery you'll see ten-thousand-gallon stainless-steel tanks for fermenting white wines. Each has a temperature-controlled environment. If left on their own, as they begin to ferment, grapes can reach a temperature of 113°F. If the grapes get too hot, instead of fermenting, the yeast starts cannibalizing the natural grape sugar and causes oxidation. A cold controlled fermentation also helps maintain the fruit character in the wine.

As music pipes in from the tasting room, other sounds, including the noise of the refrigeration and the pumping of wine, fill the air, along with the smell of wine,

Sales of wine-related items? Yes, including local and other specialty food products, logo glasses, shirts, books, dishes, and glassware.

Picnics and Programs
Picnic area open to the public? Yes.

Picnic ingredients sold in Tasting Room? Yes, including cheese, crackers, olives, a large selection of Sonoma-produced condiments, bottled water, Sonoma Sparkler, pistachios, and chocolate.

Special events or wine-related programs? Russian River Wine Road Winter Wineland in January; Wine & Chocolate Fantasy in February; Russian River Wine Road Barrel Tasting in March; Concerts on the Green May – October; open house in November. Call winery or check website for a detailed schedule of the many events.

especially when it is being racked in the barrel cellar. Here, hundreds of American and French oak barrels and Czechoslovakian oak storage tanks are used for aging red wines. Trained coopersmiths are on staff to keep the oak barrels conditioned. After about five years a barrel begins to lose its impact. To extend the barrel's use, the cooper shaves away the wood and retoasts it. The average barrel can take a maximum of five reshavings and toastings. An informative display shows how this is done.

In contrast to the dim light of the surrounding wine wings, the tasting room is bright and the bar is lit by a skylight. There is always something going on here. A chocolate party before Valentine's Day, a tasting of one of the foods sold in the tasting room, the release of a new wine, a summer concert, or a special weekend wine discount keep this winery one of the liveliest in the county. With a commitment to making all their wine from Sonoma-grown grapes, the Klein family continues to build upon the dream of the founder.

# Resources

# Sonoma County Grapes and Wines

*Suggested Sonoma County food pairing in italics.*

**Barbera:** A hearty red grape from the Piedmont region of Italy that used to be widely planted in Sonoma. Now Sebastiani and a few others are the only producers. Flavor is rich and tannic rather than fruity.

*Angelo's (Petaluma) or Willowside (Santa Rosa) sausages with Sonoma Mustard & Condiment Company (in the town of Sonoma) Cracked Brown Mustard.*

**Burgundy:** A generic term for red wine in the United States, not to be confused with wine from the French region, Bourgogne. Most producers are substituting "Red Table Wine" for the old designation. Flavor can run from dry to slightly sweet.

*Traverso (Santa Rosa) or Healdsburg Charcuterie sandwiches.*

**Cabernet Franc:** A popular grape for blending with Cabernet Sauvignon; over 500 acres are planted in Sonoma where the other Bordeaux varietals thrive, such as on Sonoma Mountain and in the Alexander Valley. Tastes lighter and more fruity than Cabernet.

*Jimtown sandwiches.*

**Cabernet Sauvignon:** Makes the world's most famous and finest wines. Known for its aging potential. Grows best on hot hillsides, which is where most of its 12,000 acres in Sonoma are located, including in Sonoma Mountain, Alexander Valley, Knight's Valley, and Russian River viticultural areas. A little is grown on the rolling hills of Los Carneros.

*Point Reyes Blue Cheese.*

**Carignane:** Less than 200 acres remain in Sonoma of this grape that was once the most common red grape in California. It does well in warm areas such as the northern Alexander Valley. The color is dark and the flavor is light.

*Downtown Bakery (Healdsburg) focaccia.*

**Chardonnay:** One of the world's finest white grapes for dry and sparkling wines, this is the white Burgundy from France. Over 15,000 acres are planted in Sonoma; the best viticultural areas are Los Carneros, Russian River, and Chalk Hill. Flavor ranges include oaky, buttery, intensely creamy, and fruity.

*Sautéed Gourmet Mushroom (Graton) shiitakes, chanterelles, and morels.*

**Chenin Blanc:** Well regarded for its light crispness and dry to honeylike sweetness, this is a white grape with a loyal but not huge following. Grown in the Alexander Valley and Chalk Hill viticultural areas.

*Curried chicken with Kozlowski Farms (Forestville) Apple Chutney.*

**Cinsault:** A red grape with full flavor and deep color, this is a Rhône variety. A few acres are planted in Sonoma, where its development and use are in experimental stages. It makes a nice Rosé.

**Fumé Blanc:** The name given to dry-style Sauvignon Blanc by Robert Mondavi in the 1960s, now used by many other producers of this popular wine. *See* Sauvignon Blanc.

**Gamay Beaujolais:** A light red wine grape that is declining in popularity in California; there are less than 200 acres planted of this relative of the popular Pinot Noir. Made in the Alexander Valley and Sonoma Valley viticultural areas.

*Bellwether Farms (Petaluma) sheep-milk cheese.*

**Gewürztraminer:** Less than 200 acres of this floral-scented grape are planted in Sonoma. The name comes from the German word for spice and refers to its aroma and flavor, which runs from dry (about 0.5 percent residual sugar) to quite sweet. A wonderful aperitif as well as a complement to spicy Asian food.

*Timber Crest Farms (Healdsburg) Sonoma Plum Duck Sauce on roasted Liberty duck.*

**Grenache:** A red grape popular in the south of France and in Spain; as the popularity of Rhône wines rises, more of this grape may be seen. Often made into dry Rosés with a slightly fruity aftertaste.

*Matos St. George cheese.*

**Johannisberg Riesling:** The true name is White Riesling; about 30 acres are planted in cool areas in Sonoma. It is a distinctively flavored grape that is the darling of many wine aficionados for its versatility in being made bone dry, in a slightly fruity style, or in an extremely sweet late-harvest version if left on the vine and attacked by the sweetness-inducing mold known as botrytis.

*Dry style with Grilled Reichardt Duck Farm (Petaluma) duck breasts. Late-harvest style with Bellwether Farms Crescenza cheese.*

**Late Harvest:** Denotes a dessert-sweet wine, whether made with Riesling, Gewürztraminer, Muscat Canelli, Semillon, Sauvignon Blanc, or Zinfandel.

*Pears, peaches, apricots, or plums from farm stands anywhere in the county.*

**Meritage:** Derived from "merit" and "heritage," this is an American designation given to wines produced in the Bordeaux style and using only the Bordeaux varieties. Red wines included: Cabernet Franc, Cabernet Sauvignon, Malbec, Merlot, and Petite Verdot. Whites: Sauvignon Blanc and Semillon. Flavors are rich, and the wines are made like reserve wines with potential for long aging.

*Vella Dry Jack cheese.*

**Merlot:** More than 7,000 acres grow in Sonoma, and more are being planted. This is the second most popular red grape in the Bordeaux and is often blended with Cabernet Sauvignon to give it more of a fruity and supple character. Grows well in the Alexander Valley, Dry Creek Valley, Sonoma Mountain, and Sonoma Valley viticultural areas.

*Piotrkowski Poultry (Petaluma) smoked duck.*

**Mourvèdre:** A red grape from the south of France with a name like a Shakespearean character. As the Rhône varietals increase in popularity in California, more of this grape will be found both blended and as a varietal. It has a deep, rich color and slightly tart flavor.

*Angelo's Meats (Petaluma) beef jerky or smoked turkey.*

**Muscat Canelli:** A white grape usually made into low-alcoholic or fortified sweet white wine. There are just under 50 acres in Sonoma County; Chateau Souverain has a few acres in front of the winery.

*Gravenstein apple pie from Mom's Pies (Sebastopol).*

**Napa Gamay:** *See* Valdiguié.

**Nebbiolo:** One of the top two red grapes in the Piedmont region of Italy (with Sangiovese), where it is known as Barolo. There are small plantings in Alexander Valley, where the Italian influence is strong. It makes a wine that is a critic's delight in roundness and complexity.

*Sonoma Cheese Factory (Sonoma) Telemé or Sonoma*

*Jack and Artisan Bakers (also in the town of Sonoma) bread.*

**Petite Sirah:** A California name given to Durif, a French grape; 400 acres of it exist in Sonoma, and many are old vines producing inky, peppery, slightly tannic wine that goes well with pasta, meat, and potatoes.

*Chargrilled beef steaks (from Niman Ranch).*

**Petite Verdot:** One of the Bordeaux five, this grape is hard to grow and is used in small amounts in blends. Geyser Peak is one winery bottling it separately to show how it tastes, which is tannic and ashy with great dark color. Not a great food wine, but interesting to sample with a little cheese.

*Vella Cheese Company (Sonoma) aged Cheddar.*

**Pinot Noir:** A versatile grape, perfect as the foundation for sparkling wine and as a varietal on its own; 10,000 acres are planted in Sonoma County. The Carneros and Russian River viticultural areas are famous for Pinot Noir, which produces full-flavored wines with the aroma and aftertaste of blackberries and raspberries.

*Broiled CK Lamb (Healdsburg) medallions.*

**Port:** A sweet fortified wine made in Sonoma County from Zinfandel and other red grapes; perfect for serving after dinner on a blustery night.

*Peter Rabbit's Chocolates (Santa Rosa).*

**Rosé:** A pink wine made from red grapes that are harvested and kept with their skins long enough to extract a little color. Usually has a fresh, fruity flavor and typically is not sweet. Rhône-style Rosé is quite dry and goes with many dishes, especially seafood and poultry.

*Roasted Willie Bird Turkey (Santa Rosa).*

**Sangiovese:** The principal grape in Italy's famous Chianti is attracting attention in Sonoma County, where nearly 500 acres have been planted. A great food wine.

*Mendocino Pasta with Timber Crest Farms (Healdsburg) Sonoma Dried Tomato Pasta Sauce.*

**Sauvignon Blanc:** California's second favorite white wine grape makes an all-purpose wine most commonly described as grassy, but that characteristic is mellowed out of most examples by various winemaking techniques and blending with Semillon. There are 2,000 acres of it all over Sonoma County. The best wines come from the Dry Creek Valley and Sonoma Valley viticultural areas.

*Grilled Rocky Range chicken.*

**Semillon:** About 200 acres of this white grape are planted in Sonoma County. The light, almost citrusy flavor makes it better for blending (with Sauvignon Blanc) than bottling as a varietal unless you count its reputation in

France, where it becomes the famous Sauternes when botrytis turns it opulently sweet for dessert wine.

*Salsa from La Casa Foods (Sonoma) or La Tortilla Factory (Santa Rosa).*

**Sparkling Wine:** If the label reads *méthode champenoise,* this is Champagne. Most wineries, in deference to the French law allowing "Champagne" on the label only if the wine comes from the Champagne region, call their bottle-fermented output "sparkling wine." Sonoma sparklers are made from blends of Chardonnay and Pinot Noir and sometimes a little Pinot Meunier. Flavors range from dry (brut) to sweet (sec and demi-sec). Sparkling wines go with any food, especially spicy flavors.

*Strawberries from Happy Haven Ranch (near the town of Sonoma); oysters from Hog Island.*

**Symphony:** A white grape original developed by the University of California at Davis; it is a cross of Grenache Gris and Muscat of Alexandria. Can be produced sweet to dry to sparkling.

*Sonoma Weisswurst sausage.*

**Syrah:** This food-friendly red wine is growing in popularity. Close to 2,000 acres are planted in Alexander Valley and other locations in Sonoma County. One of the Rhône varietals, it is the darling of a group of winemakers known as the Rhône Rangers. Flavors have peppery and black currant characteristics.

*Laura Chenel (near the town of Sonoma) aged chèvre.*

**Valdiguié:** A grape from the French Midi, it is known as Napa Gamay in California and there are about 230 acres planted in Sonoma. The flavor is light, with a balance of fruit and acid. A good all-purpose quaffing wine.

*Mezzetta Brand olives (in the town of Sonoma) and Mezzaluna Bakery (Santa Rosa) European breads.*

**Viognier:** A white Rhône varietal of which very little is planted worldwide. About 220 acres grow in Sonoma County, and its popularity is growing. The taste runs from dry with a hint of peaches and apricots to tart like grapefruit. It has the distinction of being blended into red Rhône wines.

*Sonoma brand (Petaluma) Salsa or Garlic Dip and Cousteaux (Healdsburg) French bread.*

**Zinfandel:** Zinfandel is known and loved as California's adopted varietal, and Sonoma is its mother. Of the more than 5,000 acres in Sonoma County, a respectable portion is "old vine," some more than a hundred years old, which is found in the Dry Creek Valley, Alexander Valley, and Sonoma Valley viticultural areas. This maturity gives great body and depth to the already spicy and berry-rich flavors of the robust wine. Pair with equally rich and robust food.

*Mendocino Pasta Company (Cotati) Garlic and Basil Rotelle with a hearty marinara sauce.*

Sources for this list include Sonoma County wineries; *The New Connoisseur's Book of California Wines,* by Norman Roby and Charles Olken; *The New Cook's Tour of Sonoma,* by Michele Anna Jordan; and *The New Frank Schoonmaker Encyclopedia of Wine,* by Alexis Bespaloff.

Many of the products listed are found in grocery stores and specialty food markets. For producers' addresses and phone numbers, call area code 707 information, check the Internet, request a list from Farm Trails, or see the Resources section.

# Resources

*Note: All resources are in the 707 telephone area code unless otherwise given.*

## WINE & CULINARY EDUCATION

Chateau St. Jean
8555 Sonoma Highway 12
Kenwood 95452
833-4134
chateaustjean.com

Copia: American Center for Food, Wine, and the Arts
500 First Street
Napa 94559
888-51-copia
copia.org

Geyser Peak Winery
22281 Chianti Road
Geyserville 95441
857-9400; 800-255-9463
geyserpeakwinery.com

J Vineyards & Winery
11447 Old Redwood Highway
Healdsburg 95448
431-3646
jwine.com

Ramekins Sonoma Valley Culinary School
450 West Spain Street
Sonoma 95476
933-0450
ramekins.com

St. Francis Winery & Vineyards
100 Pythian Road
Santa Rosa 95409
833-4668
stfranciswine.com

Santa Rosa Junior College Culinary Training Center
458 B Street
Santa Rosa 95401
527-4011; 800-564-7752
santarosa.edu

Sonoma County Grape Growers Association
P.O. Box 1959
Sebastopol 95473
829-3963
scgga.com

Sonoma County Wine Library
Healdsburg Regional Library
139 Piper Street
Healdsburg 95448
433-3772
sonoma.lib.ca.us/wine/index.html

## HISTORICAL SITES

Bartholomew Memorial Park
Old Winery Road
P.O. Box 311
Sonoma 95476
938-2244

Cloverdale Historical Museum
215 N. Cloverdale Boulevard
Cloverdale 95425
894-2067
cloverdalehistoricalsociety.org

Fort Ross State Historic Park Highway 1 (12 miles north of Jenner)
P.O. Box 123
Duncan Mills 95430
847-3286
parks.sonoma.net/fortross/html

General Mariano Guadelupe Vallejo's Home
West Spain at 3rd Street West
Sonoma 95476
parks.sonoma.net/sonoma.html

The Healdsburg Museum
221 Matheson Street
Healdsburg 95448
431-3325
healdsburgmuseum.org

Jack London State Historic Park
2400 London Ranch Road
Glen Ellen 95442
938-5216
jacklondonpark.com

Luther Burbank Home & Garden
Santa Rosa Avenue at Sonoma Avenue
P.O. Box 1678
Santa Rosa 95402
524-5445
lutherburbank.org

Luther Burbank's Gold Ridge Farm
7781 Bodega Avenue
Sebastopol 95473
wschs-grf.pon.net/bef.html

Mission San Francisco de Solano
20 East Spain Street
Sonoma 95476
938-1519
californiamissions.com

Petaluma Adobe State Park (General Vallejo's 1836 home)
3325 Adobe Road
Petaluma 94954
762-4871
parks.sonoma.net/adobe.html

Sonoma County Museum
425 Seventh Street
Santa Rosa 95401
579-1500
sonomacountymuseum.com

## VISITOR'S CENTERS & TOURING INFORMATION

Cloverdale Wine & Visitors Center
105 North Cloverdale Avenue
Cloverdale 95425
894-0810
cloverdale.net

Sonoma County Farm Trails
P.O. Box 6032
Santa Rosa 95406
800-207-9464; 571-8288
farmtrails.org

Sonoma County Tourism Program
520 Mendocino Avenue, Suite 210
Santa Rosa 95401
565-5380
sonomacounty.com

Sonoma Valley Visitors Bureau
453 First Street E
Sonoma 95476
996-1090
sonomavalley.com

## WINE & FOOD EVENTS LISTINGS

Alexander Valley Winegrowers
P.O. Box 248
Healdsburg 95448
888-289-4637
alexandervalley.org

Art Trails of Sonoma County
P.O. Box 7400
Santa Rosa 95407
579-2787
arttrails.org

Rhône Rangers
P.O. Box 1229
Sonoma 95476
939-8014
rhonerangers.org

Russian River Valley Winegrowers
P.O. Box 16
Fulton 95439
521-2534
rrvw.org

Russian River Wine Road
P.O. Box 46
Healdsburg 95448
433-4335; 800-723-6336
wineroad.com

Sonoma County Culinary Guild
P.O. Box 6191
Santa Rosa 95406
sonomacountyculinaryguild.org

Sonoma County Farm Markets
110 Valley Oakes Drive
Santa Rosa 95409
538-7023

Sonoma County Harvest Fair
P.O. Box 1536
Santa Rosa 95402
545-4203
harvestfair.org

Sonoma County Wineries Association
5000 Roberts Lake Road
Rohnert Park 94928
586-3795
sonomawine.com

Sonoma Valley Vintners & Growers Alliance
17964 Sonoma Highway
Sonoma 95476
935-0803
sonomavalleywine.com

Wine Brats
P.O. Box 5432
Santa Rosa 95402
877-545-3539
winebrats.org

Winegrowers of Dry Creek Valley
P.O. Box 1796
Healdsburg 95448
433-3031
wdcv.com

ZAP (Zinfandel Advocates & Producers)
P.O. Box 1487
Rough and Ready 95975
530-274-4900
zinfandel.com

## BOOKS

Ash, John. *Cooking One-on-One, Private Lessons from a Master Teacher.* New York: Clarkson Potter, 2004.

Ash, John. *From the Earth to the Table.* New York: Dutton/Penguin Group, 1995.

Jordan, Michele Anna. *The New Cook's Tour of Sonoma.* Seattle: Sasquatch Books, 2000.

Sullivan, Charles. *Zinfandel: A History of a Grape and Its Wine.* Berkeley and Los Angeles: University of California Press, 2003.

## PERIODICALS

*North Bay Bohemian*
216 E. Street
Santa Rosa 95404
527-1200
bohemian.com

*The Petaluma Post*
P.O. Box 493
Petaluma 94953
762-3260
petalumapost.com

*The Press Democrat*
P.O. Box 569
Santa Rosa 95402
546-2020
pressdemocrat.com

*The Sonoma Index Tribune*
P.O. Box C
Sonoma 95476
938-2111
sonomanews.com

Sonoma West Publishers
*Healdsburg Tribune*
*Windsor Times*
*Sonoma West Times & News*
P.O. Box 521
Sebastopol 95473
823-7845
sonomawest.com

*Spotlight's Wine Country Guide*
5 Kenilworth Court
Novato 94945
413-898-7908
winecountryguide.com

*Wine Business Journal*
5550 Skylane Boulevard, Suite B
Santa Rosa 95403
579-2900
busjrnl.com

*Wine Country Living*
489 First Street West
Sonoma 95479
935-0111
winecountryliving.net

*Wine Country This Week*
255 W. Napa Street, Suite P
Sonoma, CA 95476

## CERTIFIED FARMERS' MARKETS

*See also*: Sonoma County Farm Bureau, cafarmersmarkets.com

Cotati
June–October
Thursday 5:00–8:30 P.M.
795-5508

Duncan Mills
April–November
Saturday 11:00 A.M.–3:00 P.M.
865-4171

Guerneville
May–September
Wednesday 4:00–7:00 P.M.
865-4171

Healdsburg
May–November
Saturday 9:00 A.M –noon
Tuesday 4:00–6:00 P.M.
431-1956

Oakmont
All year
Saturday 9:00 A.M –noon
538-7023

Occidental
May–November
Saturday 9:00 A.M –12:30 P.M.
874-2242

Petaluma
May–October
Saturday 2:00 P.M.–5:00 P.M.
762-0344

Santa Rosa Downtown
May–August
Wednesday 5:00–8:30 P.M.
524-2123

Santa Rosa Fairgrounds
All year
Wednesday & Saturday
8:30 A.M –noon
523-0962

Sebastopol
April–Thanksgiving
Sunday 10:00 A.M –1:30 P.M.
522-9305

Sonoma
All year
Friday 9:00 A.M –noon
538-7023

Windsor
June–August
Thursday 5:00–8:00 P.M.
May–October
Sunday 10:00 A.M –noon
829-3494

## MAJOR WINE & FOOD EVENTS CALENDAR

### January

Russian River Wine Road
Winter Wineland
800-723-6363
wineroad.com

Sonoma Valley Olive Festival
935-4383
sonomavalley.com

### February

Cloverdale Citrus Fair
894-3992
cloverdale.net

Sonoma Valley Olive Festival
935-4383
sonomavalley.com

### March

Heart of the Valley Barrel Tasting
800-543-7713
heartofthevalley.com

Russian River Wine Road
Barrel Tasting
800-723-6363
wineroad.com

### April

Apple Blossom Festival
877-828-4748
sebastopol.org

Butter & Egg Days Parade
769-0429
visitpetaluma.com

Winegrowers of Dry Creek
Passport Weekend
433-3031
wdcv.com

### June

Alexander Valley
Winegrowers
Taste of the Valley
431-2894
alexandervalley.org

### July

Salute to the Arts
P.O. Box 1947
752 Broadway
Sonoma 94599
salutetothearts.com

Sonoma County Showcase &
Wine Auction
586-3795
sonomawine.com

### August

Russian River Winegrowers
Grape to Glass
546-3276

Sonoma Valley Harvest
Wine Auction
935-0803
sonomavalleywine.com

### October

Harvest Fair
545-4203
sonomacountyfair.com

### November

Russian River Wine Road
A Wine & Food Affair
800-723-6363
wineroad.com

### December–February

Sonoma Valley Olive Festival
935-4383
sonomavalley.com

# A Directory of Sonoma County Wineries

*Note: Bold denotes wineries profiled in this book. All are area code 707, unless otherwise given.*

*Tasting room addresses are given where appropriate. Visit websites for more information. If no website is listed, there wasn't one at press time.*

A. Rafanelli Winery
4685 W. Dry Creek Road
Healdsburg 95448
433-1358
arafanelliwinery.com

Abundance Vineyard
5700 Occidental Road
Santa Rosa 95401
544-7876
abundancevineyards.com

Acorn Winery/Alegria
  Vineyards
12040 Old Redwood
  Highway
Healdsburg 95448
433-6440; 888-228-7676
acornwinery.com

Adler Fels Winery
5325 Corrick Lane
Santa Rosa 95405
539-3123
adlerfels.com

Albini Family Vineyards
886 Jensen Lane
Windsor 95492
838-9249

Alderbrook Winery
2306 Magnolia Drive
Healdsburg 95448
433-5987; 800-405-5987
alderbrook.com

Alexander Valley Vineyards
8644 Highway 128
Healdsburg 95448
800-888-7209
avvwine.com

Amphora Winery
3901 Wine Creek Road
Healdsburg 95448
431-7767
amphorawines.com

Annapolis Winery
26055 Soda Springs Road
Annapolis 95412
886-5460
annapoliswinery.com

Archipel & Verité Wines
4611 Thomas Road
Healdsburg 95448
800-296-1952

Arista Winery
5 Fitch Street
Healdsburg 95448
473-0606
aristawinery.com

Armida Winery
2201 Westside Road
Healdsburg 95488
433-2222
armida.com

Arrowood Vineyards
  & Winery
14347 Sonoma Highway
Glen Ellen 95442
938-510; 800-938-5170
arrowoodvineyards.com

Balletto Vineyards
5700 Occidental Road
Santa Rosa 95401
568-2455
ballettovineyards.com

Bandiera
155 Cherry Creek Road
Cloverdale 94525
942-9721
bandiera.com

Barefoot Cellars
420 Aviation Boulevard
Santa Rosa 95403
524-8000
barefootwine.com

Bartholomew Park Winery
1000 Vineyard Lane
Sonoma 95476
935-9511
bartholomewparkwinery.com

Battaglini Estate Winery
2948 Piner Road
Santa Rosa 95401
578-4091
battagliniwines.com

Belvedere Vineyards
  & Winery
4035 Westside Road
Healdsburg 95448
800-433-8296, ext. 442
belvederewinery.com

**Benziger Family Winery**
1883 London Ranch Road
Glen Ellen 95442
935-3000
benziger.com

Blackstone Winery
8450 Sonoma Highway
Kenwood 95452
833-1999
blackstonewinery.com

Braren Pauli Winery
1611 Spring Hill Road
Petaluma 94592
778-0721
brarenpauli.com

B.R. Cohn
15140 Sonoma Highway
Glen Ellen 95442
938-4064
brcohn.com

**Buena Vista Winery**
18000 Old Winery Road
Sonoma 95476
938-1266; 800-926-1266
buenavistawinery.com

Camellia Cellars
57 Front Street
Healdsburg 95448
433-1290
camelliacellars.com

Canyon Road Winery
19550 Geyserville Avenue
Geyserville 95441
800-793-9463
canyonroadwinery.com

Castle Vineyards
1105 Castle Road
Sonoma 95476
996-4188
castlevineyards.com

Cecchetti-Sebastiani Cellars
P.O. Box 1887
Sonoma 95476
933-1704

Chalk Hill Estate Vineyards
  & Winery
10300 Chalk Hill Road
Healdsburg 95448
838-4306
chalkhill.com

Chandelle of Sonoma
P.O. Box 2167
Glen Ellen 95442
938-5862
chandellewinery.com

Charles Creek Vineyard
Sonoma Wine Company
919 Graton Road
Graton 95444
996-6622
charlescreek.com

Chateau Felice
10603 Chalk Hill Road
Healdsburg 95448
chateaufelice.com

**Chateau St. Jean**
8555 Sonoma Highway 12
Kenwood 95452
833-4134
chateaustjean.com

Chateau Souverain
400 Souverain Road,
P.O. Box 528
Geyserville 95441
433-3141; 888-80-WINES
chateausouverain.com

Christopher Creek Winery
641 Limerick Lane
Healdsburg 95448
433-2001
christophercreek.com

**Cline Cellars**
24737 Highway 121
Sonoma 95476
935-4310
clinecellars.com

Clos du Bois
19410 Geyserville Avenue
Geyserville 95441
857-3100; 800-222-3189
closdubois.com

Collier Falls
9931 W. Dry Creek Road
Healdsburg 95448
433-7373
collierfalls.com

Copain Wine Cellars
1160B Hopper Avenue
Santa Rosa 95403
541-7474

Crane Canyon Cellars
Locals Tasting Room
Geyserville Road at
  Highway 128
Geyserville 95441
575-3075
tastelocalwine.com

David Bruce Winery
21439 Bear Creek Road
Los Gatos 95033
408-354-4214;
800-397-9972
davidbrucewinery.com

David Coffaro Vineyard
 & Winery
7485 Dry Creek Road
Geyserville 95441
433-9715
coffaro.com

Davis Bynum Winery
8075 Westside Road
Healdsburg 95441
433-2611; 800-826-1073
davisbynum.com

Deerfield Ranch Winery
Family Wines of Sonoma
9200 Sonoma Highway 12
Kenwood 95452
833-5504

Dehlinger
6300 Guerneville Road
Sebastopol 95472
823-2378

DeLoach Vineyards
1791 Olivet Road
Santa Rosa 95401
526-9111
deloachvineyards.com

de Lormier Winery
2001 Highway 128
Geyserville 95441
857-2000; 800-546-7718
delormierwinery.com

DeNatale Vineyards
11020 Eastside Road
Healdsburg 95448
431-8460
denatel@cds1.net

Deux Amis Winery
1960 Dry Creek Road
Healdsburg 95448
431-7945

Domaine Danica Winery
1960 Dry Creek Road
Healdsburg 95448
431-1902
domainedanica.com

Domaine St. George Winery
1141 Grant Avenue
Healdsburg 95448
433-5508
domainesaintgeorge.com

Dreyer-Sonoma
P.O. Box 484
Graton 95444
650-851-9448
dreyerwine.com

**Dry Creek Vineyard**
3770 Lambert Bridge Road
Healdsburg 95448
433-1000; 800-864-WINE
drycreekvineyard.com

Dutton-Goldfield Winery
P.O. Box 527
Sebastopol 95472
823-3887
duttongoldfield.com

Dynamite Vineyard
1 Vintage Lane
Glen Ellen 95442
823-3887
dynamitevineyard.com

Eric Ross Winery
13404 Dupont Road
Occidental 95465
874-3046

Estancia Vineyards
P.O. Box 407
Rutherford 94573
963-7111
estanciaestates.com

Everett Ridge Vineyards
 & Winery
435 W. Dry Creek Road
Healdsburg 95448
433-1637
everettridge.com

Favero Vineyards & Winery
3939 Lovall Valley Road
Sonoma 95476
935-3939

**Ferrari-Carano Vineyards**
 **& Winery**
8761 Dry Creek Road
Healdsburg 95448
433-6700
ferrari-carano.com

**Field Stone Winery**
10075 Highway 128
Healdsburg 95448
433-7266; 800-54-GRAPE
fieldstonewinery.com

Fisher Vineyards
6200 St. Helena Road
Santa Rosa 95404
539-7511
fishervineyards.com

Flowers Vineyard & Winery
28500 Sea View Road
Cazadero 95421
847-3661
flowerswinery.com

**Foppiano Vineyards**
12707 Old Redwood
 Highway
Healdsburg 95448
433-7272
foppiano.com

Forchini Vineyards
 & Winery
5141 Dry Creek Road
Healdsburg 95448
431-8886
forchini.com

Forth Vineyards
Locals Tasting Room
Geyserville Avenue at
 Highway 129
Geyserville 95441
473-0553
forthvineyards.com

Frei Brothers Winery
12707 Old Redwood
 Highway
Healdsburg 95448
431-5545
freibrothers.com

Frick Winery
23072 Walling Road
Geyserville 95441
857-3205

**Fritz Winery**
24691 Dutcher Creek Road
Cloverdale 95425
894-3389; 800-418-9463
fritzwinery.com

Gallo of Sonoma
320 Center Street
Healdsburg 95448
431-5500; 433-2458
gallosonoma.com

Gan Eden Winery
4950 Ross Road
Sebastopol 95472
829-5686
ganeden.com

Gary Farrell Wines
10701 Westside Road
Healdsburg 95448
473-2900
garyfarrellwines.com

**Geyser Peak Winery**
22281 Chianti Road
Geyserville 95441
857-9400; 800-255-9463
geyserpeakwinery.com

Gladstone Cellars
The Tasting Room
21043 Geyserville Avenue
Geyserville 95441
473-9637

**Gloria Ferrer Champagne**
 **Caves**
23555 Highway 121
Sonoma 95476
996-7256
gloriaferrer.com

Goldridge Pinot
P.O. Box 749
Sebastopol 95473
829-2031
goldridgepinot.com

Grove Street Winery
1451 Grove Street
Healdsburg 95448
433-0290
grovestreetwinery.com

**Gundlach-Bundschu Winery**
2000 Denmark Street
Sonoma 95476
938-5277
gunbun.com

Hafner Vineyard
P.O. Box 1038
Healdsburg 95448
433-4606

Hanna Winery
Hospitality Center
9280 Highway 128
Healdsburg 95448
431-4310
hannawinery.com

Hanna Winery
Tasting Room
5353 Occidental Road
Santa Rosa 95406
575-3371; 888-426-6288
hannawinery.com

Hartford Family Winery
8075 Martinelli Road
Forestville 95436
887-1756
hartfordwines.com

Hart's Desire Wines
25094 Asti Road
Cloverdale 95425
579-1687

Hawley Wine
6387 West Dry Creek
Healdsburg 95448
431-2705

Haywood Winery
498 First Street East
Sonoma 95476
939-0579
haywoodwinery.com

Holdredge Wine
51 Front Street
Healdsburg 95448
431-1424
holdredge.com

Homewood Winery
23120 Burndale Road
Sonoma 95476
996-6353
homewoodwinery.com

**Hop Kiln Winery**
6050 Westside Road
Healdsburg 95448
433-6491
hopkilnwinery.com

Huntington Wine Cellars
53 Front Street
Healdsburg 95448
433-5215
huntingtonwine.com

Icaria Creek Winery
27750 Asti Road
Cloverdale 95425
894-8499
icariawinery.com

Imagery Estate Winery
14335 Highway 12
Glen Ellen 95442
935-4500; 877-660-4278
imagerywinery.com

**Iron Horse Vineyards**
9786 Ross Station Road
Sebastopol 95472
887-1507
ironhorsevineyards.com

**J Vineyards & Winery**
11447 Old Redwood
  Highway
Healdsburg 95448
431-3646
jwine.com

Johnson's Alexander Valley
  Winery
8333 Highway 128
Healdsburg 95448
433-2319
johnsonwine.com

Jordan Vineyard & Winery
1474 Alexander Valley Road
Healdsburg 95448
431-5250; 800-654-1213
jordanwinery.com

Joseph Swan Vineyards
2916 Laguna Road
Forestville 95436
573-3747
swanwinery.com

Kaz Winery
233 Adobe Canyon Road
Kenwood 95452
833-2536
kazwinery.com

Keller Estate
5875 Lakeville Highway
Petaluma 94954
765-2117
kellerestate.com

Kendall-Jackson Wine
Center
5007 Fulton Road
Fulton 95439
571-8100
kj.com

Kendall-Jackson Wine
Country Store
337 Healdsburg Avenue
Healdsburg 95448
433-7102
kj.com

Kenwood Vineyards
9592 Sonoma Highway
Kenwood 95452
833-5891
kenwoodvineyards.com

**Korbel Champagne Cellars**
13250 River Road
Guerneville 95446
824-7000
korbel.com

**Kunde Estate Winery**
  **& Vineyards**
10155 Sonoma Highway 12
  Kenwood 95452
833-5501
kunde.com

La Crema Winery
Tasting at Kendall-Jackson
337 Healdsburg Avenue
Healdsburg 95448
433-7102
lacrema.com

Lake Sonoma Winery
9990 Dry Creek Road
Geyserville 95441
473-2999; 800-750-9463
lakesonomawinery.net

Lambert Bridge Winery
4085 West Dry Creek Road
Healdsburg 95448
431-9600; 800-975-0555
lambertbridge.com

Lancaster Estate Winery
15001 Chalk Hill Road
Healdsburg 95448
433-8178; 800-799-8444
lancasterestate.com

Landmark Vineyards
101 Adobe Canyon Road
Kenwood 95452
833-0053; 800-452-6465
landmarkwine.com

Laurel Glen Vineyard
P.O. Box 548
Glen Ellen 95442
526-3914
laurelglen.com

Laurier Winery
20580 Eighth Street
Sonoma 95476
938-3220

Ledson Winery & Vineyards
7335 Sonoma Highway 12
Kenwood 95452
833-2330
ledson.com

Limerick Lane Cellars
1023 Limerick Lane
Healdsburg 95448
433-9211

Lost Canyon Winery
(western Sonoma)
1017 22nd Avenue #300
Oakland 94606
650-341-6577
lostcanyonwinery.com

Loxton
P.O. Box 70
Glen Ellen 95442
935-7201
loxtoncellars.com

Lynmar Winery
3909 Frei Road
Sebastopol 95472
829-3374
lynmarwinery.com

MacMurray Ranch
9015 Westside Road
Healdsburg 95448
431-5507
macmurrayranch.com

MacPhail Wines
851 Magnolia Drive
Healdsburg 95448
433-4780
macphailwines.com

Martinelli Winery
3360 River Road
Windsor 95492
535-0570
martinelliwinery.com

Martin Family Vineyards
P.O. Box 1532
Healdsburg 95448
433-9545
martinfamilyvineyards.com

Martin Ray Winery
2191 Laguna Road
Santa Rosa 95401
823-2404
martinray-winery.com

**Matanzas Creek Winery**
6097 Bennett Valley Road
Santa Rosa 95404
528-6464; 800-590-6464
matanzascreek.com

Mayo Family Winery
Family Wines of Sonoma
  Valley
9200 Sonoma Highway 12
Kenwood 95452
833-2883
mayofamilywinery.com

Mazzocco Vineyards
1400 Lytton Springs Road
Healdsburg 95448
431-8159
mazzocco.com

McCray Ridge
1960 Dry Creek Road
Healdsburg 95448
433-2932
mccrayridge.com

The Meeker Vineyard
21305 Geyserville Avenue
Geyserville 95441
431-2148
meekervineyards.com

Meredith Wine Cellar/
  Merry Edwards Wines
Family Wines of Sonoma
9200 Sonoma Highway 12
Kenwood 95452
838-9950; 888-388-9050
merryedwardswine.com

Michel Schlumberger
4155 Wine Creek Road
Healdsburg 95448
433-7427; 800-447-3060
michelschlumberger.com

Mill Creek Vineyards
  & Winery
1401 Westside Road
Healdsburg 95448
431-2121
mcvonline.com

Mojon's Bench
647 Lytton Station Road
Geyserville 95441
415-431-9147

Moondance Cellars
The Wine Room
9575 Sonoma Highway 128
Kenwood 95452
moondancecellars.com

Moon Mountain Vineyards
1700 Moon Mountain Drive
Sonoma 95476
996-5870
chalonewinegroup.com

Murphy-Goode Estate
  Winery
4001 Highway 128
Geyserville 95441
431-7644
murphygoodewinery.com

Nalle Winery
P.O. Box 454
Healdsburg 95448
433-1040
nallewinery.com

Nelson Estate Vineyards
Family Wines of Sonoma
  Valley
9200 Sonoma Highway 12
Kenwood 95452
833-5504
nelsonestate.com

Noel Wine Cellars
Family Wineries of Sonoma
  Valley
9200 Sonoma Highway 12
Kenwood 95452
833-5504

Optima Wine Cellars
498C Moore Lane
Healdsburg 95448
431-8222

Papapietro-Perry Winery
4441 Westside Road
Healdsburg 95448
433-0422
papapietro-perry.com

Paradise Ridge Winery
4545 Thomas Lake
Harris Drive
Santa Rosa 95403
528-9463
paradiseridgewinery.com

Paul Hobbs
3355 Gravenstein Highway
Sebastopol 95472
824-9879
paulhobbswinery.com

Pedroncelli Winery
1220 Canyon Road
Geyserville 95441
857-3531; 800-836-3894
pedroncelli.com

Pellegrini Family Vineyards
4055 W. Olivet Road
Santa Rosa 95404
575-8463; 800-891-0244
pellegrinisonoma.com

Peter Michael Winery
12400 Ida Clayton Road
Calistoga 94515
942-4459
petermichaelwinery.com

Peterson Winery
1040 Lytton Springs Road
Healdsburg 95448
431-7568
petersonwinery.com

Pezzi King Vineyards
241 Center Street
Healdsburg 95448
431-9388; 800-411-4758
pezziking.com

Pfendler Vineyards
P.O. Box 4958
Petaluma 94955
765-5997
pfendlervineyards.com

Porter Creek Vineyards
8735 Westside Road
Healdsburg 95448
433-6321
portercreekvineyards.com

**Preston of Dry Creek Winery
  & Vineyards**
9282 West Dry Creek Road
Healdsburg 95448
433-3372; 800-305-9707
prestonvineyards.com

Pride Mountain Vineyards
4900 St. Helena Road
Santa Rosa 95404
963-4949
pridewines.com

**Quivira Estate Vineyards
  & Winery**
4900 West Dry Creek Road
Healdsburg 95448
431-8333; 800-292-8339
quivirawine.com

Rabbit Ridge Winery
3291 Westside Road
Healdsburg 95448
431-7128
rabbitridgewinery.com

Rancho Zabaco Winery
3387 Dry Creek Road
Healdsburg 95448
431-5681
ranchozabaco.com

**Ravenswood Winery**
18701 Gehricke Road
Sonoma 95476
933-2332
ravenswood-wine.com

Raymond Burr Vineyards
8339 West Dry Creek Road
Healdsburg 95448
433-4365; 888-900-0024
raymondburrvineyards.com

Rezonja Wine Cellars
1684 Canyon Road
Healdsburg 95448
431-1449
rezonjawinecellars.com

Ridge Vineyards/
  Lytton Springs
650 Lytton Springs Road
Healdsburg 95448
433-7221
ridgewine.com

Robert Hunter
15655 Arnold Drive
Sonoma 95476
996-3056

Robert Rue Vineyard
1406 Wood Road
Fulton 95439
578-1601
robertruevineyard.com

Robert Stemmler Winery
498 First Street East
Sonoma 94576
939-0579
robertstemmlerwinery.com

Robert Young Estate Winery
4960 Red Winery Road
Geyserville 95441
431-4811
ryew.com

Robledo Family Winery
21901 Bonness Road
Sonoma 95476
939-7040
robledofamilywinery.com

Roche Carneros Estate
  Winery
28700 Highway 120
Sonoma 95476
935-7115
rochewinery.com

Rochioli Vineyards
  & Winery
6192 Westside Road
Healdsburg 95448
433-2305

**Rodney Strong Vineyards**
11455 Old Redwood
  Highway
Healdsburg 95448
431-1533
rodneystrong.com

Rosenblum Cellars
250 Center Street
Healdsburg 95448
431-1169
rosenblumcellars.com

Roshambo Winery
3000 Westside Road
Healdsburg 95448
433-7165; 888-251-9463
roshambowinery.com

Russian Hill Estate Winery
4525 Slusser Road
Windsor 95492
575-9428
russianhillwinery.com

Rutz Cellars
3637 Frei Road
Sebastopol 95472
823-0370
rutzcellars.com

Sable Ridge Vineyard
Family Wines of Sonoma
9200 Sonoma Highway 12
Kenwood 95452
sableridge.com

**St. Francis Winery
  & Vineyards**
100 Pythian Road
Santa Rosa 95409
833-4668
stfranciswine.com

Sapphire Hill Vineyards
51 Front Street
Healdsburg 95448
431-1888
sapphirehill.com

Sausal Winery
7370 Highway 128
Healdsburg 95448
433-2285; 800-500-2285
sausalwinery.com

Schug Carneros Estate
 Winery
602 Bonneau Road
Sonoma 95476
939-9363; 800-966-9365
schugwinery.com

**Sebastiani Vineyards
 & Winery**
389 Fourth Street
Sonoma 95476
933-3230; 800-888-5532
sebastiani.com

Sebastopol Vineyards–
 Dutton Estate
8757 Green Valley Road
Sebastopol 95472
829-9463
sebastopolvineyards.com

**Seghesio Family Vineyards**
14730 Grove Street
Healdsburg 95448
433-3579
seghesio.com

Selby Winery
5 Fitch Street
Healdsburg 95448
431-1703
selbywinery.com

Siduri Wines
980 Airway Court, Suite C
Santa Rosa 95403
578-3882
siduri.com

Silver Oak Cellars
 Alexander Valley
24625 Chianti Road
Geyserville 95441
857-3562; 944-8808
silveroak.com

**Simi Winery**
16275 Healdsburg Avenue
Healdsburg 95448
800-746-4880
simiwinery.com

Skewis Pinot Noir
P.O. Box 1895
Headlsburg 95448
431-2160
skewiswines.com

Smothers/Remick Ridge
The Wine Room
9575 Sonoma Highway 12
Kenwood 95452
833-1010; 800-795-WINE
smothersbrothers.com

Sonoma Creek Winery
23355 Millerick Road
Sonoma 95476
938-3031
sonomacreek.com

Sonoma-Cutrer Vineyards
4401 Slusser Road
Windsor 95492
528-1181
sonomacutrer.com

Stonestreet Winery
337 Healdsburg Avenue
Healdsburg 95448
433-7102
stonestreetwines.com

Stone Creek
9380 Sonoma Highway 12
Sonoma 95452
833-5070
stonecreekwines.com

Stryker Sonoma Vineyards
 & Winery
5110 Highway 128
Geyserville 95441
433-1944; 800-433-1944
strykersonoma.com

Stuhlmuller Vineyards
4951 West Soda Rock Lane
Healdsburg 95448
433-7745
stuhlmullervineyards.com

Sullivan Birney Winery
 & Vineyards
13647 Arnold Drive
Glen Ellen 95442
533-8514
sb-ranch.com

Suncé Vineyard & Winery
1839 Olivet Road
Santa Rosa 95401
526-9463
suncewinery.com

Suncé Vineyard & Winery
Family Wines of Sonoma
9200 Sonoma Highway 12
Kenwood 95452
833-5504

Taft Street Winery
2030 Barlow Lane
Sebastopol 95472
823-2049; 800-334-8238
taftstreetwinery.com

Tara Bella Winery
3701 Viking Road
Santa Rosa 95401
544-9049; 877-698-9463
tarabellawinery.com

F. Teldeschi Winery
5017 Dry Creek Road
Healdsburg 95448
433-1283
teldeschi.com

Thurow Vineyards
3393 Dry Creek Road
Healdsburg 95448
433-9729
thurowvineyards.com

Toad Hollow Vineyards
409A Healdsburg Avenue
Healdsburg 95448
431-8667; 888-856-4889
toadhollow.com

Topolos at Russian River
 Vineyards
5700 Gravenstein Highway N
Forestville 95436
887-1139; 800-TOP-OLOS
topolos.com

Trecini Vineyards
1107 Sonoma Avenue
Santa Rosa 95405
528-8668

Tremani Vineyards
3420 Guerneville Road
Santa Rosa 95401
544-8877
tremaniwines.com

**Trentadue Winery**
19170 Geyserville Road
Geyserville 95441
433-3104
trentadue.com

Unti Vineyards & Winery
4202 Dry Creek Road
Healdsburg 95448
433-5590
untivineyards.com

Valley of the Moon Winery
777 Madrone Road
Glen Ellen 95442
996-6941
valleyofthemoonwinery.com

Venus Vineyard
3279 Westside Road
Healdsburg 95448
473-9600

**Viansa Winery &
 Italian Marketplace**
25200 Arnold Drive
Sonoma 95476
800-995-4740
viansa.com

Vision Cellars
P.O. Box 1756
Windsor 95492
837-8593
visioncellars.com

VJB Vineyards & Cellars
9077 Sonoma Highway 12
Kenwood 95452
833-2300
vjbcellars.com

Wattle Creek Winery
25510 River Road
Cloverdale 95425
894-5166
wattlecreek.com

Wellington Vineyards
11600 Dunbar Road
Glen Ellen 95422
938-0708
wellingtonvineyards.com

White Oak Vineyards
 & Winery
7505 Highway 128
Healdsburg 95448
433-8429
whiteoakwines.com

Williams-Selyem
850 River Road
Fulton 95439
433-6425
williams-selyem.com

Wilson Winery
1960 Dry Creek Road
Healdsburg 95448
433-4355
wilsonwinery.com

Windsor Vineyards
308B Center Street
Healdsburg 95448
433-2822; 800-204-9463
windsorvineyards.com

Yoakim Bridge Winery
7209 Dry Creek Road
Healdsburg 95448
433-8511
yoakimbridge.com

# Index